D0887359

WETHERSFIELD INSTITUTE

Proceedings, 1992

WHEN CONSCIENCE AND
POLITICS MEET:
A CATHOLIC VIEW

When Conscience and Politics Meet: A Catholic View

Papers Presented at a Conference
Sponsored by the Wethersfield Institute
New York City, October 16, 1992

IGNATIUS PRESS   SAN FRANCISCO

Cover by Riz Boncan Marsella

Cover art: *Sir Thomas More*
by Hans Holbein
© The Frick Collection, New York

Published 1993, Ignatius Press, San Francisco
ISBN 0-89870-477-4
Library of Congess catalogue number 93-78818
Printed in the United States of America

WETHERSFIELD INSTITUTE
STATEMENT OF PURPOSE

The purpose of Wethersfield Institute is to promote a clear understanding of Catholic teaching and practice, and to explore the cultural and intellectual dimensions of the Catholic Faith. The Institute does so in practical ways that include seminars, colloquies and conferences especially as they pursue our goals on a scientific and scholarly level. The Institute publishes its proceedings.

It is also interested in projects that advance those subjects. The Institute usually sponsors them directly, but also joins with accredited agencies that share our interests.

Msgr. Eugene V. Clark, President
E. Lisk Wyckoff, Jr., Vice President
Patricia Puccetti Donahoe, Program Director

CONTENTS

CONTRIBUTORS

WILLIAM BENTLEY BALL, ESQ., is a constitutional lawyer in the firm Ball, Skelly, Murren & Connell in Harrisburg, Pennsylvania.

MARY ELLEN BORK is a distinguished lecturer in Washington, D.C.

REV. FRANCIS CANAVAN, S.J., is Professor Emeritus, and a Political Scientist at Fordham University, New York.

JAMES HITCHCOCK is Professor of History at St. Louis University, St. Louis, Missouri.

RUSSELL HITTINGER is Professor of Philosophy at Catholic University, Washington, D.C.

RUSSELL KIRK is a distinguished seminal thinker and writer from Mecosta, Michigan.

MSGR. EUGENE V. CLARK

PREFACE

The Wethersfield Institute, dedicated to exploring Catholic intellectual and cultural questions, found the subject of politics and conscience irresistible.

And it is an important subject today because conscience-in-politics is, in many circles, a slogan more than a demanding question.

It is not patronizing to discern in our society a lack of interest in binding conscience. Oddly the media is full of allusions to conscience which, it turns out, is largely sentiment. And sentiment rarely rises to discover intellectual bases for conscience that clarify reality, specify norms, and lead to conviction.

But there are good signs. Many persons of high ideals and personal integrity want to be precise in speaking of their obligations and loyalties, of committing themselves to principle, of appreciating ethical essentials. They long for intellectual firmness and reliable language.

They also sense the comfort of sharing motives with other men and women of integrity, and adhering to carefully defined principles—principles for which, in some cases, a person may be prepared to die. To be hazy there is a scary business.

Conscience is also a *rich* notion. Many enriching factors influence a refined conscience: wisdom drawn from history; experience of human nature; a capacity to weigh the consequences of political, cultural, or popular changes in society; prudence in method; discipline in self-seeking . . . these and much else may inform conscience.

The believing Christian knows more; namely, that the grace of God enlightens conscience when human wisdom loses focus. Conscience so enlightened bespeaks a morality resting on God's protective love.

God's moral code is especially needed for the protection of human beings from political practice. The Emperor Franz Joseph of Austria-Hungary once said his role was to "protect his people from their government". He gives us pause. In your name the Wethersfield Institute expresses its gratitude to the philosophers and political scientists who created these insightful papers on conscience and politics: William Bentley Ball, Esq.; Mrs. Mary Ellen Bork; Father Francis Canavan S.J.; Dr. James Hitchcock; Dr. Russell Hittinger; and Dr. Russell Kirk.

And I thank Patricia Puccetti for her unfailing competence in organizing our conference and seeing the papers into print.

RUSSELL KIRK

CHURCH ESTABLISHMENTS
AND AMERICAN CATHOLICS

I take it, Ladies and Gentlemen, that the complex subject as-
signed to me is meant to be confined to the Catholic experience in the United States, and does not touch upon the national
churches by law established during the Protestant Reformation.
Let me commence, then, by quoting to you the first clause—
or, as some would have it, two clauses—of the First Amendment to the Constitution of the United States, prohibiting the
establishment by the Congress of a national church:

> "Congress shall make no law respecting an establishment of
> religion, or prohibiting the free exercise thereof. . . ."

We are concerned here with the history and present effect of
that clause upon the Catholic Church in this land; which clause
began as a protection for religious observance and a broad toleration, but recently has come down to an intolerance by federal
courts that forbids, among other matters, baccalaureate sermons
at public-school commencement exercises.

Since the 1820s, the remnants of church establishments in
the several states of the Union have been swept away; and
earlier, Episcopalian establishments this side of the Atlantic
had vanished during the Revolution or shortly thereafter. This
abolition generally was approved by American Catholics, who
formed a small minority in every one of the original Thirteen
States, and therefore were relieved by the First Amendment
from any peril of adverse discrimination or active persecution
by the general government. The "establishment clause" of the

First Amendment, therefore, coincided with American Catholics' interests and convictions. For evidence of this sentiment, we may turn to the most eminent of American Catholic laymen during the Revolutionary era, Charles Carroll of Carrollton, the Maryland statesman, who at Maryland's constitutional convention in 1776 drafted a bill of rights. Here is the draft of Declaration 35: "No person ought to be by any law molested in his person or estate for his religious persuasion, profession, or practice, nor compelled to frequent or maintain, or contribute, unless on contract, to any religious worship, place of worship, or ministry." And in Declaration 34, the text of the draft read, "The rights of conscience are sacred, and all persons professing the Christian religion ought to ever enjoy equal rights and privileges in the state." Doubtless Carroll remembered his own family's experience of adverse religious discrimination against Catholics.

American Catholics' ready acceptance of such prohibitions of state churches in the federal Constitution and in most state constitutions, however, was not merely in consequence of the expedient protection of their communion, which this doctrine of civil liberty obviously promised; for separation of church and state was a very old Catholic doctrine. Thirteen centuries earlier, Pope Gelasius I had enunciated the doctrine of the Two Swords: "Two there are by whom this world is ruled."

Many people who ought to know better still write and speak of the first clause of the First Amendment as if the separation of church and state were an eighteenth-century American invention, perhaps sprung full-armed from the brow of James Madison. In truth, the demarcation of authority between secular rule and spiritual rule had its origins in disputes between the Latin Church and the Byzantine state at the end of Roman times. In every century since then—in every generation, one might almost say—church and state have fallen into conflict, in some degree, in West or East. But it is not of violent persecution that I speak today. Rather, we are immediately concerned with less ferocious contests, in our country, that result from differing interpretations of the first clause of the First Amendment.

The Framers who drew up this amendment, James Madison of Virginia and Fisher Ames of Massachusetts (then members of the House of Representatives), had two intentions: first, to ensure religious toleration, so far as the federal government was concerned, lest sectarianism become divisive in the infant Union; second, to prevent Congress from interfering with the Congregational churches, already by law established in several New England states, or with any other churches that other states might choose to re-establish.

The first clause of the First Amendment never was meant to signify that the American national government was indifferent to religion or hostile toward it. Justice Joseph Story, in his *Commentaries on the Constitution* (1833), gave a clear explanation of this clause, which prohibited the establishment of a *national* church. "Probably at the time of the adoption of the Constitution, and of the First Amendment. . . ." Story wrote, "the general if not the universal sentiment in America was that Christianity ought to receive encouragement from the state so far as was not incompatible with the private rights of conscience and the freedom of religious worship. An attempt to level all religions, and to make it a matter of state policy to hold all in utter indifference, would have created universal disapprobation, if not universal indignation."

Religion in America never has been merely a private concern. It is religious belief, indeed, that has made the American democracy successful; as Alexis de Tocqueville pointed out, the lack of religious foundations has been the ruin of other democracies.

But in recent years, a confusing series of decisions in federal courts has left many people puzzled as to what "separation of church and state" now signifies in this country. The doctrine of Chief Justice Burger that "entanglement" of church and state must be averted has been carried by some other Supreme Court justices to lengths disapproved by Mr. Justice Burger while he still presided over the Supreme Court. In particular, church-related schools have encountered severe difficulties with both state and federal public agencies. Let me offer you, very succinctly, an account of such controversies at law.

For a century and more, the Establishment Clause of the Constitution created no difficulties for churches and church schools, and did not interfere with the policies of state governments in such matters. Hostility between state and church was not suggested. As Professor T. M. Cooley wrote in the 1896 edition of his *General Principles of Constitutional Law*, "It was never intended that the government should be prohibited from recognizing religion . . . where it might be done without causing any invidious distinctions between religious beliefs, organizations or sects." Until well into the twentieth century, courts applied the First Amendment only to the federal government; it was not intended to make the states subservient to restraints placed upon the United States Congress by the Constitution.

Throughout the nineteenth century, American courts generally assumed that there subsisted a close connection between American public institutions and the Christian moral order. Take the ruling of the Supreme Court in the case of *The Late Corporation of the Church of Jesus Christ of the Latter Day Saints v. the United States* (1891): "The organization of a community for the spread and practice of polygamy is, in a measure, a return to barbarism. It is contrary to the spirit of Christianity and of the civilization which Christianity has produced in the Western world."

But this old relationship between the American political order and the Christian moral order has been changing over the past seven decades. Increasingly, although not consistently, the United States Supreme Court has held that the provisions of the Bill of Rights, the first Ten Amendments, now are binding upon the several States—or at least some of those Amendments, some of the time. Historical justification of this argument is shaky; some scholars and judges contend that the courts may not enlarge the operation of the Bill of Rights without authorization of Congress, or perhaps a constitutional amendment. Chief Justice Rehnquist is of the number of these jurists.

Out of the application of the First Amendment to the several States has arisen a mass of litigation and increasing interference with the public schools and public concerns generally by both federal courts and federal administrative agencies. Ever since 1947, when the Supreme Court enunciated in the case of *Everson v. Board of Education* a doctrine of absolute separation of state and church (*à la* Thomas Jefferson's "wall of separation") courts have tended to push religious knowledge and observances out of public schools and public concerns generally. The long series of decisions, beginning in the 1950s, about prayer in public schools, Bible-reading, quotation of certain religious references from certain public documents, display of the Decalogue on school walls, even a moment of silence in schools (for who could tell whether the little wretches might then be praying privately?), even the presence of a Bible on school shelves or in a teacher's desk, even a mention of God at a public school commencement exercise—why, those decisions, to employ a phrase frequently used by the courts about other concerns, have exerted a chilling effect. Any reference to the transcendent, or even to prescriptive morals, has been driven out of most public schools.

In *obiter dicta* the Supreme Court suggested that schools still might take up the history of religion, comparative religions, and similar subjects, short of imparting dogma. But school boards, school administrators, and nearly all teachers, shuddering at the possibility of lawsuits by militant-atheist parents or other "Separation" zealots, speedily purge themselves of any odor of sanctity. Down the Memory Hole with religion!

Now the trouble with purging school curricula of religious knowledge is that *ultimate* questions cannot be answered without reference to religious beliefs. Eliminate Christian belief, Jewish belief, and all the rest—and one leaves a vacuum. Nature abhorring vacuums, something different rushes in to fill the cavity—ferocious ideology, perhaps.

Now what has all this lamentation over school curricula to do with the question of established churches? Why, this: that we confront the grim possibility of a new establishment of religion, or of anti-religion, established not so much by law as by judges. Already this question of a bellicose establishment of secularism has arisen in federal courts. The label commonly applied to this new religion or quasi-religion is "secular humanism", a term apparently drawn from Christopher Dawson's writings. A more accurate name for it might be "humanitarianism". Permit me here a digression by way of definition.

During the past thirty years and more, the place which religion used to hold in American schooling (always a rather modest and non-dogmatic place, incidentally) has been filled by this body of belief we call *secular humanism* or *humanitarianism*. (The latter word signifies the belief that human nature and society may be perfected without the operation of divine grace). During the 1930s, John Dewey and his colleagues founded the American Humanist Association for purposes not at all humane, in the old sense of the words "humanism" and "humanities". It was the aspiration of the subscribers to the Humanist Manifesto to sweep away the old order, spiritual and temporal, and to establish a Brave New World, rejecting the superstitions of traditional religion, and bringing about egalitarian social patterns.

This humanitarianism, or secular humanism (not to be confounded with the Christian Humanism of Erasmus or Sir Thomas More, nor yet with the New Humanism or American Humanism of Irving Babbitt and Paul Elmer More in the 1920s and 1930s) of the school of Dewey amounted to what philosophers and historians of religion call "a secular religion". The Humanist Manifesto of 1933 (often called by John Dewey the Religious Humanist Manifesto) declares that the universe is self-existing, not created; that science shows the unreality of supernatural sanctions for human values; that this earthly existence is the be-all and end-all for any individual, so far as mankind can know; that religious emotions are best expressed in heightened personality and in efforts to advance social well-being; that Man himself is maker and active power, unmoved by transcendent forces.

In the book *A Common Faith* (1934), Dewey advocated his brand of humanism as a religion. "Here are all the elements for a religious faith that shall not be confined to sect, class, or race", he wrote. "Such a faith has always been implicitly the common faith of mankind. It remains to make it explicit and militant."

It is this non-theistic religion, hostile to much of the established morality and some existing American institutions that has come close to being established as a "civil religion" in American public schools. And pressures already exist to persuade or compel Christian schools to conform to this quasi-religion of humanitarianism.

Now since 1947, the Supreme Court has been handing down decisions purporting to prevent "entanglement" of church and state, especially with respect to the subject of religion in schools. (Parenthetically, one must remark that many judges now on the federal bench seem strongly affected themselves by the doctrines of secular humanism.) But the Supreme Court repeatedly has affirmed that the state's neutrality with respect to religion does not signify that federal or state governments may favor a militant secularism in schools.

Judges still cite the opinion of Justice William O. Douglas in the *Zorach* case (1952). Douglas reasoned that to hold that government must not encourage religious instruction, "would be to find in the Constitution a requirement that the government show callous indifference to religious groups. That would be preferring those who believe in no religion over those who do believe. . . . But we find no constitutional requirement which makes it necessary for government to be hostile to religion and to throw its weight against efforts to widen the effective scope of religious influence." And a footnote in the *Schempp* case (1963) affirms that "the State may not establish 'a religion of secularism' in the sense of affirmatively opposing or showing hostility to religion. . . ."

Yet militant secularists have contrived since *Schempp*, very cleverly, to employ certain powers of the judiciary, the educational apparatus, and the bureaucracy to diminish the influence of religious groups. This militantly secular mentality, strident in the popular media of communication, book publishing, and universities and colleges, undermines the moral order of the country.

How does this aggressive secularism direct the actions of the government? Of the American people, about half are in communion with some church, or at least attend services with some regularity; while of the other half of the population, few are consciously hostile toward religion. If anywhere in the world Christian belief might be expected to inform public policy, it is in this country.

Nevertheless, for three decades major decisions of the federal courts, especially with respect to schools, have run counter to the desires and interests of Christian churches and parents. And so it has gone, too, with juridical rulings about abortion, pornography, and a congeries of other concerns involving moral judgments. Public prayer becomes juridically suspect, at best —nay, even the reading aloud of public documents in which the Supreme Being is mentioned. In many states, adoption of children can be arranged only through a state agency; "no fault divorce" contributes to the decay of the family; "consenting adults" are permitted to behave as nastily as they choose; special privileges are granted to homosexuals; every foulness is indulged on cable television; a pretended zeal for the "privacy" of female children leads to the invalidating of penalties for "statutory rape": all this "liberation" and more besides accomplished during the past three decades.

It may be said that these court decisions, and similar measures authorized by new federal or state statutes and regulations, have to do with morals, rather than with religious belief; and that nobody proposes to interfere with worship, so long as religious believers do not thrust their opinions into public affairs. No doubt; but that is cold comfort. In so reduced a condition, churches seem ineffectual and archaic. The militant secularists may count upon a fairly rapid rate of attrition among religious believers, what with the character of instruction in schools and the pervasive influence of television, films, and salacious publications.

Need we labor such points? I am seeking merely to suggest why courts, Congress, state legislatures, city and county councils, and other public bodies seem obedient frequently to the adversaries of the church visible. How is it that the state, in this democratic American society, has been persuaded to scowl, if somewhat furtively, upon the church?

The answer, I suppose, is that most of the time, in most matters, our American Republic is ruled by minorities—that is, by vigorous, well-financed pressure groups, intent upon objectives in public policy of peculiar advantage to the minority in question. During the 1970s, the most powerful lobby in Washington and in every state capital was not that of some manufacturers' association or of the AFL-CIO, but of the National Education Association (with its state affiliates), hard opponents of any sort of concession to private and church-related schools. And there exist other lobbies, such as People for the American Way, that endeavor strenuously to oppose religious concerns in public affairs.

This observation brings us to the case of *Douglas T. Smith, et al. v. Board of School Commissioners of Mobile County*—argued in 1986, a public-school case. I was a witness for the federal district court in that trial, being summoned chiefly to offer definitions of the term "humanism". Perhaps everybody present today has read newspaper accounts—which almost without exception were confused and erroneous accounts —of the issues involved in Judge Brevard Hand's court at Mobile.

Judge Hand found in favor of the plaintiffs, Christian parents who objected to certain textbooks in social studies and in home economics prescribed for use in Mobile's public schools, because they discriminated against religious convictions or thoughtfully excluded information about religions. For this Judge Hand has been fantastically reviled by the militant secularists.

Hand concluded in his opinion that "for the purposes of the First Amendment, secular humanism is a religious belief-system, entitled to the protection of, and subject to the prohibitions of, the religion clauses. It is not a mere scientific methodology that may be promoted and advanced in the public schools."

The "values clarification" and "moral development" systems advocated by certain of the textbooks used in Mobile Schools, Judge Hand found, are based upon quasi-religious concepts, and stand in contradiction of the assumptions of transcendent religions such as Christianity and Judaism. "Teaching that moral choices are purely personal and can only be based on some autonomous, as yet undiscovered and unfulfilled, inner self is a sweeping fundamental belief that must not be promoted by the public schools," Judge Hand remarked. "With these books, the State of Alabama has overstepped its mark, and must withdraw to perform its proper non-religious functions."

After examining the home economics books in question, and receiving expert testimony about them, Judge Hand declared, "The books teach that the student must determine right and wrong based only on his own experience, feelings, and 'values.' These 'values' are described as originating from within. . . . This faith assumes that self-actualization is the goal of every human being, that man has no supernatural attributes or component, that there are only temporal and physical consequences for man's actions, and that these results, alone, determine the morality of an action. This belief strikes at the heart of many theistic religions' beliefs that certain actions are in and of themselves immoral, *whatever the consequences*, and that, in addition, actions will have extra-temporal consequences."

My own testimony in the case was quoted by Judge Hand in his opinion, to the effect that what is called "secular humanism" indeed has developed into a religion or anti-religion, hostile toward the religions of transcendence. In conformity to the First Amendment, Judge Hand reasoned, the state must not impose a nontheistic religion upon public schools, any more than it may impose a particular theistic religion. The Judge's own words put the principle well: "If this court is compelled to purge 'God is great, God is good, we thank Him for our daily food' from the classroom, then this court must also purge from the classroom those things that serve to teach that salvation is through man's self rather than through a deity."

In short, the textbook trial at Mobile was a clear case of conflict between people who believed in teachings of the church —as expressed in the Apostle's Creed, say—and other people who believed public instruction to be a means for the triumph of views militantly secular—or, at best, a "civil religion". The Court of Appeals overturned Judge Hand's decisions, and the plaintiffs shrank from the cost and trouble of appealing to the Supreme Court of the United States.

I hope, ladies and gentlemen, that I have not been a Pied Piper, leading you into a Minoan maze of litigation where you wander despairing. In that Mobile courtroom, between examinations and cross-examinations, I meditated upon Orestes Brownson's essay "The Higher Law", published on the very eve of the Civil War, in which he demonstrates that in the collision between the state's positive law and the radicals' private interpretation of the law of nature, "We have an infallible Church to tell us where there is a conflict between the human and the Divine"—a Church that can mediate and reconcile the claims of Authority and the claims of personal Freedom. Beneath that Church's foundations, in the closing decades of the twentieth century, the militant secularists lay their petards, and call upon the state to aid them.

Everything in private life and in public affairs, I think, depends upon how you and I answer this ultimate question: do we have souls, or do we not? The tendency of course, in recent years, has been to assume that we do not have souls, or rather that we aren't souls. If that mechanistic and materialistic illusion is permitted to triumph, in the long run there will be no human bodies, either; for life becomes not worth living, then, except in a narcotic trance or a monkey-like sexuality; and society falls apart—"The center cannot hold / mere anarchy is loosed upon the world."

However this may be, it is not too late for us to proclaim once more that this world is ruled by two authorities, not one merely; and that the City of God ought not to be confounded with the City of This Earth. I do not trust self-righteous zealots as political economists; but neither do I trust members of Congress as infallible arbiters of wisdom and virtue.

I have been commending, in short, the venerable Christian understanding of the division of sovereignty between the spiritual authority and the political authority. As the sagacious Father John Courtney Murray wrote three decades ago, "Christianity has always regarded the state as a limited order of action for limited purposes, to be chosen and pursued under the direction and correction of the organized social conscience of society, whose judgments are armed and mobilized by the Church, an independent and autonomous community, qualified to be the interpreter of man's nature and destiny." But, as Father Murray wrote in the same chapter of his book *We Hold These Truths*, "Over the whole of modern politics there has hung the monist concept of the indivisibility of sovereignty: 'One there is.'"

The informed Christian knows that a political order uninformed by a spiritual order must go down to dusty death; and so it is coming to pass in our time. We still may utter the teaching that T. S. Eliot, in his drama *Murder in the Cathedral*, puts upon the lips of St. Thomas à Becket:

> *Those who put their faith in worldly order*
> *Not controlled by the order of God,*

In confident ignorance, but arrest disorder,
Make it fast, breed fatal disease,
Degrade what they exalt.

Much of the litigation in which schools have been unhappily involved during recent years is bound up with the discarding of belief in transcendence by people in high places—in the Congress, on the bench, in the universities. It is even conceivable that the visible Church, sued to death, may end not with a bang, but a whimper.

Should that catastrophe occur, the triumphant secularists soon would discover that a domination allegedly humanitarian would be anything but humane. I call these troubles to your attention, my friends, because we ought to remind ourselves of the admonition, "Say not the struggle naught availeth", and to be heartened by a line from Chesterton's long poem *The Ballad of the White Horse*: "But men marked of the cross of Christ go gaily in the dark."

Russell Hittinger

IS THERE A POLITICAL HOME
FOR CATHOLICS IN AMERICA?

I. A View from 1960

In 1960 there was good reason to believe that American Catholics were poised for a "Catholic Moment". On the eve of the election of the first Catholic president, Catholics had come a long way since the early, agrarian years of the Republic. The first census of 1790 showed that Catholics comprised a mere one percent of the population. By 1960, some thirty-five million Catholics represented the largest religious denomination in the country. They had not only mastered the art of municipal politics, but also proved to be the driving force of the largest electoral coalition of modern times, Roosevelt's "New Deal". Compared with their grandparents, Catholics in 1960 were better educated and wealthier. If a political home meant access to the instruments of civil power and economic prosperity, then Catholics were certainly at home by 1960.

That year, in Rome, the preparatory commissions and secretariats were at work planning the Second Vatican Council. At least by American perceptions, the Church hardly appeared to be in decline. Catholics had resisted religious assimilation. First, the Church presented a clear and unyielding position on marriage. Inter-religious marriages were almost always resolved, not just *de jure* but also *de facto*, in favor of the Catholic spouse. Second, the Church built an extensive system of parochial education. By 1960, it contained 3,500,000 elementary school children, 700,000 in secondary school, and 300,000 students in colleges and universities. Even as cautious an observer of

American things as Christopher Dawson would write in 1961 that the parochial school system represented "a record of voluntary effort which I believe has no parallel in the world."[1]

1960 marked the publication of John Courtney Murray's *We Hold These Truths*.[2] Although the book was only a set of collected essays, it provided a sophisticated explanation of what many Catholics already knew at the practical level: namely, that the Catholic mind could be reconciled with what Murray called the American "proposition". Indeed, as Catholics looked around them in 1960, they found that the civil institutions were sound. Just three years earlier, a young Catholic Supreme Court justice from New Jersey, William Brennan, wrote his first important majority opinion, rejecting First Amendment protection of obscenity.[3] Justice Brennan did not invoke any specifically Catholic propositions. It sufficed to invoke the "universal judgment" of nations, as well as the history of anti-obscenity laws in the forty-eight states. Although the Court recently had started down the road of interpreting the Establishment Clause according to a doctrine of strict separation,[4] it had not yet gone so far as to remove generic, civil religion from the public schools.[5] In fact, in 1960 one-third of the nation's schools began the school day with a prayer, and forty-two percent required Bible readings.[6]

Catholics enthusiastically supported American legal institutions. They not only were eagerly recruited by law-enforcement agencies like the FBI, but also could be found on the forefront of the legal prosecution of Communists and mobsters. While Catholic law schools came nowhere near the prestige of the Ivy League, such schools as Fordham and Notre Dame trained thousands of lawyers who practiced law throughout the legal and political regime. With respect to the federal judiciary, Jacques Maritain wrote in 1958: ". . . I think that the American institution of the Supreme Court is one of the great political achievements of modern times, and one of the most significant tributes ever paid to wisdom and its right of pre-eminence in human affairs."[7]

II. Consensus and American Exceptionalism

Maritain, however, went even further in his expression of enthusiasm for the American situation: ". . . we may believe that if a new Christian civilization, a new Christendom is ever to come about in human history, it is on American soil that it will find its starting point."[8] This sentiment was based in large part on his estimation of the moral structure of American political institutions. Maritain, along with many other Catholic intellectuals of the day, believed that it was the civilized world's great fortune that the imperial power of the mid-twentieth century should believe in limited, constitutional government, based ultimately upon principles of natural law. This was a comparably rare dispensation in world history. Indeed, Maritain thought that the American experiment provided a model for the international community of nations recuperating from the wars.[9]

In *Man and the State* (1951), Maritain outlined the philosophical case for "a common secular faith in the democratic charter."[10] The democratic charter, he argued, rests upon a practical rather than a theoretical consensus about the principles which ought to animate the civil order. He wrote:

> Thus it is that men possessing quite different, even opposite metaphysical or religious outlooks, can converge, not by virtue of any identity of doctrine, but by virtue of an analogical similitude in practical principles, toward the same practical conclusions, and can share in the same practical secular faith, provided that they revere, perhaps for quite diverse reasons, truth and intelligence, human dignity, freedom, brotherly love, and the absolute value of moral good.[11]

The important point for our purposes is that Maritain believed that this consensus is precisely what had been achieved in America, where a pluralistic democracy cohered because of its common practical faith in the natural law of rights.[12] The issue of the day was not whether Catholics had a political home in the material and instrumental sense of the term, but rather whether the moral "form", or what Murray termed the "propositions", of the American *civitas* agreed with the Catholic mind. Could the spiritual children of John Locke and Pius IX constitute a common civil order, notwithstanding dissensus about doctrinal and speculative matters? For Maritain, America gave living, historical testimony to the feasibility of this ideal.

Other Catholic intellectuals of the era, such as John Courtney Murray, Yves Simon, and Christopher Dawson subscribed to the position, which, for lack of a better term, we can call the doctrine of "American exceptionalism".[13] I borrow the term from a recent essay by William Gould on the work of John Courtney Murray. Gould, it should be noted, worries that "American exceptionalism" was due less to the actual historical record than to Murray's effort to fashion "a noble myth".[14] Only in America, it seemed, did Catholics enjoy citizenship in a constitutional order, of the modern sort, without having to re-fight the French Revolution. The "myth" would have us believe that the American founding, as well as its subsequent history, evince a consensus about first things more or less uninfected by those aspects of the Enlightenment that the Church justifiably fought, tooth and nail, in Europe. But even if the doctrine of American exceptionalism was a noble myth —a high reading of the American founding unsupported by history—it was a myth that was being coined in the mind of more than one theorist.[15]

Christopher Dawson, for example, observed that although the Enlightenment in Europe divided the political community on matters of first principles, "in America it meant the coming of an age of faith—the establishment of a doctrine which united the whole people in allegiance to certain common truths."[16] For Dawson, the political problem of modern Europe could be traced to its rejection of natural law and the ideal of a constitutionally limited state.[17] Seen in this light, it was plausible to say that America preserved what Europe had lost. Thus, Christopher Dawson, who was ever the Eurocentrist on education, recommended that Catholic schools in America should emphasize the natural law tradition. This tradition, he observed, is in the American bones, and represents a point of connection with the older, Catholic view of the moral basis of government.[18] Here, the Catholic has immediate access to the civil conversation about the principles of government. It was in this same spirit that John Courtney Murray would write: "Where this kind of language is talked," that is, natural law, "the Catholic joins the conversation with complete ease. It is his language."[19]

The doctrine of American exceptionalism led not merely to the notion that there is a happy suitability between American institutions and the pre-modern, Catholic mind of the Old World. The doctrine also suggested an agenda. Since Catholics in the United States did not have to contest the first principles of civil order, the intellectual and moral wisdom of Catholicism could be used to deepen and ennoble the civil institutions. It is important for us to remember that although Catholic intellectuals like Murray, Maritain, Dawson, and Simon shared the conviction that a moral wisdom was embedded in the institutions and practices of the American civil order, they were not particularly impressed with the philosophies home-grown on these shores. While respectful of the Protestant religious background of the American practice of liberty, they also saw that Protestantism was at low tide. The secular philosophies which remained were inferior to the older Protestant vision of moral and political order. Indeed, one who re-reads Murray's *We Hold These Truths* today is struck not only by how critical, but how openly disdainful he was of American intellectual culture—both past and present.[20]

Perhaps it was a Catholic conceit to believe that the Sage of Monticello should be read according to the philosophy of the Angelic Doctor, just as it was perhaps a conceit of the Jewish neo-classical thinkers to think that Abraham Lincoln should be interpreted through the lens of the Greeks. But these ideas were widely accepted and intelligently articulated in that earlier "Catholic moment" of 1960. In summary, the position espoused by pre-conciliar liberals (and more recently by post-conciliar neo-conservatives), is that Catholics in America enjoy the unique blessing of not having to engage in either open or covert warfare with the regime over matters of first principles. This being assumed, Catholics can move on to the cultural mission of ennobling and deepening the intellectual and moral habits of their fellow citizens.

Today, the obvious point to be made is that things have changed since 1960. Who could have predicted that the Supreme Court would rule that the right unilaterally to kill the unborn is a fundamental proposition of American "liberty"? Or that a clear majority of Americans, by roughly equal percentages, would say that abortion is murder, but that government must defer to the choice of the woman? Or that parents would be forbidden by the law from knowing that their children are having abortions, or being instructed in the use of mint-flavored condoms, even when these things are being done by or through the offices of the state itself? Or that a black, educated in Catholic schools in the rural South, would have his nomination to the Supreme Court threatened because he gave a speech agreeing with Lincoln's understanding of the natural law basis of the Constitution? Who would have thought that a Catholic justice of the Supreme Court would write an opinion saying that public schools violate constitutional order when they have non-denominational prayers at graduation exercises because these prayers, according to the Catholic justice, drain secular events of their meaning?[21]

III. The Meaning of the Political

Our real interest is not in compiling a list of these tribulations and woes, but rather in how to think about them. At the root we find the same question posed by Murray and Maritain: *Not* whether Catholics have a material home in American politics, but whether the principles constituting the civil order are acceptable to Catholics. Looking at the question from our point in time, can we still answer it affirmatively?

Trained in the tradition of scholastic philosophy, Maritain and Murray understood that Aristotle was right when he taught that first principles must be presupposed, and therefore are not amenable to direct debate. These principles stand at two levels. First, they are the formal principles of the *ordo juris* which constitute the civil sphere, entitling it to act in the name of the people, and to receive their obedience. Second, they consist in the unwritten habits and practices of our common institutional life; that is, in the habits whereby the formal principles are held and made ready for common action.

Today, for the first time in memory, Catholics find themselves having to contest the first principles of the civil polity. To the extent that this has become a reality, it is no longer true that Catholics have a political home. Note that I say "to the extent that". Like disease, dissensus about first principles is something that admits of degrees. No one is able to discern with confidence the inner moral life of another human person, much less the intersubjective world of social bodies. Rather, like laymen in medical matters, we are constrained to read the gross symptoms. The symptoms, however, are clear.

Increasingly, the citizens today find themselves addressing problems of the civil order through partisan uses of power, unmediated by agreement about first things. Indeed, the political rhetoric of the major parties evinces a desperate attempt to hide the fact that disagreement has now reached the first principles themselves. It seems that only the powers and the tools of politics remain. But, of course, politics is no more an issue simply of power, than piano playing is simply a matter of pressing piano keys. Power only deserves the name "political" when it is exercised for the common good, on the basis of principles commonly recognized by the governed and those who govern. Where power is exercised unmediated by consensus about these principles, there politics has ceased.

In order to clarify what it means to be engaged in the political sphere, we can briefly consider a case in which the properly political element is missing altogether. Consider, if you will, everyone's favorite example of a corrupt regime—Hitler's Germany. A Catholic of good conscience in this regime necessarily found himself having to contest the first principles of the civil order. It makes no difference that many Catholics didn't—the point is that a good Catholic should have done so. In the Third Reich, the problem was not a mistaken application of the first principles of civil government; nor was it a policy question of means toward ends; nor, finally, was it simply a case of a "culture war" within different parts of the German population. Rather, it was a perversion of those principles which entitle a corporate power to be regarded as a *civitas*. Hence, the citizen of good conscience enjoyed no political means to contest the perversion of first principles. There was no option but to resist the state.

As Catholics in Eastern Europe could explain perfectly well, to be in such a situation is to have no political home. For there to be a political home, in any genuine meaning of the term, one must be able to exercise judgment *qua* citizen through the mediation of civil institutions, in accord with the publicly recognized and morally justified principles of law. Without the context of just civil institutions, one may be exercising the proper acts of a human moral agent; one might be deploying instruments of power; and one might even be exercising a certain prophetic office; but one cannot be said to be acting in the role of citizen. In short, one can have a linguistic home, a material home, and even in some broad meaning of culture a cultural home, without having a political home.

As I said, this problem admits of degrees. I began with the extreme example only to clarify the idea that there is a proper meaning to politics. One can like the same cinemas as everyone else; one can speak the same language; one can, from time to time, acquire tools of power; one can even have the franchise to vote; and still have no political home.

In order to illustrate this point by way of a less extreme example, let us recall the condition of the black community in America at the middle point of this century. Here, we had a people bound to the rest of the country by common language, religion, and popular culture. But many sectors of the law regarded them as inferior, either as to their humanity or as to their participation in the civil order. For good reason, the black community engaged in the tactic of civil disobedience. They could not pretend they were citizens while acquiescing in a civil order that subverted the very basis of their citizenship; that is, a civil order that exacted, in exchange for some elements of citizenship, a tacit concession of their *de jure* inferiority vis-à-vis the rest of the civil community. Civil rights leaders understood that black Americans had to resist the temptation to exchange real citizenship for the material benefits of being cabaret stars and sports celebrities. Nor would it suffice to manipulate the levers of power to get the succor of government with respect to material benefits. Welfare, after all, could be given to individuals who have no citizenship. Nor, finally, would it do to invoke the empty liberal notion that they had a right not to think of themselves as inferior, by a kind of private choice.

It was the good fortune of all concerned that the black community was able to successfully appeal to the conscience of the citizens, and to resolve the political issue without a protracted series of non-political acts. I submit that this was a case in which the first principles of civil consensus at the institutional and habitual level were sufficiently intact to permit a resolution of the argument at the formal, juridical level. The country came to see that racial discrimination was not only unfair to blacks, but as such was a flaw in the legal regime itself.

Catholics today, however, are in a more perilous position with regard to the problem of abortion. Whereas Martin Luther King could appeal to the residual moral habits of the people, it is no longer clear that this resource is available in the debate over abortion. Moreover, we are more thoroughly assimilated; we are materially prosperous; we cannot claim immediate or obvious civil disabilities; and the perversions of civil order that threaten their citizenship are not infrequently perpetrated by Catholics in public office. All of this makes it difficult for Catholics to summon their moral voice in the situation.

IV. Political Heresy

The situation is this: because of abortion the American polity has fallen into political heresy. This heresy should not be defined merely in Catholic terms. Rather, it bespeaks an abandonment of the first principles of the civil order. It takes away from Catholics and non-Catholics alike the very presuppositions on which moral conscience can be reconciled with the political institutions.

Why call abortion "political heresy"? For the sake of clarity about this important issue, it might be helpful first to adopt the *via negativa*, and say what is not "political heresy". In the first place, the fact that some, or for that matter, many individuals acting in a private capacity allow themselves to act contrary to moral law is not in itself a regime-threatening issue. We can imagine a situation in which the moral habits of the people are at such a low ebb that we would not want to live around these people. We can also imagine how an erosion of morality will lead, in time, to a corruption of the formal juridical principles of politics. But until such time that the principles of the political state are corrupted, we cannot speak of "political heresy".

In the second place, in the matter of abortion we are not dealing with governmental toleration of wicked acts. Were this the case, the Catholic community would disagree with the policies, but not necessarily the principles, of the government. Of course, as the Vietnam War era made clear, disputes over policies can have serious moral ramifications for the state. Yet even if the acts of a government are morally flawed with respect to what is deliberately tolerated or promoted via official policies, this can be distinguished from a moral flaw in the principles informing the institutions of the government.

In the third place, abortion does not present us with the problem of interstices or loopholes in the law which indirectly afford legal protection to morally wicked acts. Once again, were this the case, we would not be bound in principle to respect an individual's right to kill the unborn, but rather would be hamstrung by legal lacunae. To be sure, a regime that failed to fix such lacunae would be a regime that deserves moral criticism, but it would not necessarily be a regime that has bound itself to the principle that individual citizens may kill the unborn.

I call abortion "political heresy" because, as it is defined by our judicial system, and as it is understood and practiced by the citizens, the right to abortion is a right to commit the action itself. As I have explained in detail elsewhere, the important development in *Planned Parenthood v. Casey* (1992) is the fact that the joint opinion moved the abortion right from privacy to liberty under section one of the Fourteenth Amendment.[22] Prior to *Casey*, the right to abortion was derived (in the judge-made law) from a broad reading of the right to marital privacy vindicated in *Griswold v. Connecticut* (1965). Virtually everyone knew that there was nothing in either the Constitution, judicial precedent, legislative history, nor in moral logic itself, that justified including abortion within the zone of marital privacy. Social and legal progressives wanted the right planted more securely in "liberty" for the good reason that they wanted it made clear, as a matter of principle, that the liberty of women to procure abortions has nothing to do with either privacy or the traditional meaning of marriage. They wanted recognition of a fundamental right to perform the action itself.

Casey has given them that victory. But the victory has consequences which cannot be ignored. In the first place, it is no longer possible to view the judge-made abortion law as an overly-broad construal of marital privacy. Under the regime of *Roe v. Wade*, we could pretend that the right of privacy, however dubious its Constitutional foundation, was at least something resembling a morally justified limit upon the state. We could pretend that the right to abortion was only a mistaken extension of an otherwise acceptable immunity from government. This benign view is no longer possible. In the second place, once government recognizes a fundamental right to perform this morally wrongful act, the *civitas* is bound to a principle. And, in the matter of abortion, that alleged principle is that a citizen may rightfully kill another human being who is in no dereliction of any moral or civil duty. It is no more or no less than a public recognition of a private franchise to commit unjustifiable homicide.

In our polity, the power of the United States government is limited in two ways: (i) by the allocation and enumeration of the powers of government, and (ii) by individual rights. It might be true that individual rights have acquired an importance out of proportion to the original mind of the framers and ratifiers of the Constitution. But this issue, as important as it is to our historical judgment, should not cause us to overlook the obvious fact. Rightly or wrongly, wisely or imprudently, the American polity has come to understand principles of justice through the logic of individual rights. For this reason, there is little margin for error.[23] Should the logic of rights be corrupted, the regime is threatened at the level of first principles.[24]

And what does the logic of rights entail? If one has a right, then it means that others are duty-bound to do or not do something with respect to the claimant. A fundamental right does not bind the action of the holder of the right, but others to whom obligation reaches. Who is bound? We are! "We", that is, insofar as we are citizens and freeholders, who deliberate and act through democratic assemblies. The alleged right to abortion, therefore, does not bind some anonymous government, but rather renders the citizens themselves duty-bound to recognize the right of those citizens who elect to abort the unborn. Thus, it is both false and useless to pretend that the moral issue is transacted in a merely private sphere, for the principle of the right binds all of the citizens as to what they may legitimately do *qua citizens*, (for example, in making and enforcing laws, in formulating policies, and in conducting any meaningful public business that touches upon the alleged right).

The Catholic conscience, or for that matter, any conscience

rightly formed, cannot be relieved by the legal fact that citizens also have a right not to kill their unborn children. Whether we elect to kill them or not, the principle stands undiminished and unqualified. For the law recognizes a civil right of individuals to commit wrongful acts of homicide, and prohibits the citizens, working through democratic assemblies, from proscribing such acts. The unborn children of parents who elect not to kill them remain in the same position vis-à-vis the law as those who are killed. They have been exempted by legal fiat from the protection of the general, standing laws against wrongful homicide.[25] Not just Catholics, but also the Protestants and Jews who came to these shores by the boatload would have been surprised to learn that when they chose not to kill their own children they were exercising the very same right as those who deliberately kill them.

We must not lose sight of the moral fact that the harm done in abortion is not merely the harm to the unborn, nor the harm done to the conscience of Catholics and other right-thinking persons who are wrongfully limited in their actions as citizens. Looking at the problem from the standpoint of the common good, abortion rights undermine the first end, if not the first act, of civil government. By transferring the power over life and death to private choice, the state violates the civil contract. In effect, the power originally invested in civil government is relinquished. For John Locke, of course, this would be tantamount to returning to a pre-civil condition, in which each individual is a judge and executor of the law of nature. If a person has a private franchise to kill other human beings on the basis of his own estimation of the human status or worthiness of those whom he kills, then why shouldn't other persons have a private franchise to kill *that* person who, in their estimation, unjustifiably committed this homicidal act? Of course, from the seed of this notion follows the dissolution of civil government.

I am certainly *not* suggesting that the moral wrong of abortion consists in the fact that it is done by private parties rather than by public officers. Rather, I am calling attention to the specifically political wrong of abortion rights. The power of lethal force does not belong to the individual citizen, except in the case of self-defense, which is not the point at issue in the abortion right. A state that juridically recognizes a transfer of this power to individual citizens is a state that dissolves its own authority; a citizen who takes that power, is no longer a citizen, but rather someone who declares himself to stand outside the civil order.

Thus, to recapitulate my argument. Abortion rights represent "political heresy" for two reasons. First, the alleged right to do this moral wrong cannot be regarded as a merely private act. For the logic of rights requires that other citizens are bound to recognize this right, and accordingly to limit their activities *as citizens*. This is a morally wrongful limit upon citizenship. No right minded citizen can accept that limit as a condition for exercising his citizenship. Second, the alleged right to abortion subverts the first act of government, which is to reserve the power of lethal force to itself. Since this power can only be used rightfully for the sake of the common good, the state has no authority to transfer it to private parties; nor do private parties have warrant to take it.

Because abortion represents not just a moral wrong, but a political heresy, it is not confineable like other private immoralities. Abortion has poisoned the political culture at nearly every level. It has required the Supreme Court to act in violation of its Constitutionally allocated powers; it has led government to permit private parties to arbitrarily define in and out of existence "persons" who are within the jurisdiction of the state; it has inclined all of the tributaries of the legal system to recognize a right to do wrong, not just in this matter but also in others—notably euthanasia, which is another case of an allegedly private franchise to kill human beings; it has corrupted the quasi-public professional organizations; it has grafted itself into the health-care system and insurance carriers; it has been funded by public monies in some of the states; and one of the two great political instruments, the Democratic Party, the traditional party of Catholics, is unequivocally committed not just to the protection of this alleged right, but to its extension.

The abortion issue is destroying the consensus upon which citizenship can be exercised—both the formal and explicit consensus regarding the rule of law, as well as the informal, and largely implicit, consensus about first things held in the habits of the people.

Thus, the analogy to the slavery issue is fitting. James Madison, a slaveholder, argued at the Constitutional convention that it would be "wrong to admit in the Constitution the idea that there could be property in men".[26] With consummate clarity, Madison saw that this principle could not be admitted without poisoning the fundamental law. Moreover, many of Madison's Southern colleagues understood that the institution of slavery would eventually lead to a corruption of both the personal and civic habits of the people. But, so long as slavery was not *de jure* a fundamental or natural right, it was open to political action to gradually eliminate its existence. It was not until late in the game, specifically in Justice Taney's opinion in *Dred Scott*, that the Constitutional order was interpreted to protect slavery as a fundamental right. At that point, the principles of civil amity and unity were destroyed. For those citizens who believed slavery to be a moral wrong were compelled, as citizens, to recognize an unrightful right (on the part of the slaveholder) and an unrightful limitation on their power as citizens in the democratic process.

The full logic of *Dred Scott* did not work itself out. The issue was resolved by a war. But had the war not intervened, citizens of the non-slave states would have witnessed not only the extension of slavery in the western states and territories, but also the Constitutional challenge to their recognition of free blacks as citizens within their own jurisdictions. Twenty years after *Roe v. Wade*, we are witnessing precisely such a juggernaut in the case of abortion.

V. What Kind of "Catholic Moment"?

Let us conclude with a passage from John Courtney Murray's *We Hold These Truths*.

> Perhaps there will one day be wide dissent even from the political principles which emerge from natural law, as well as dissent from the constellation of ideas that have historically undergirded these principles—the idea that government has a moral basis; that the universal moral law is the foundation of society; that the legal order of society—that is, the state—is subject to judgment by a law that is not statistical but inherent in the nature of man; that the eternal reason of God is the ultimate origin of all law; that this nation in all its aspects—as a society, a state, an ordered and free relationship between governors and governed—is under God. The possibility that widespread dissent from these principles should develop is not foreclosed. If that evil day should come, the results would introduce one more paradox into history. The Catholic community would still be speaking in the ethical and political idiom familiar to them as it was familiar to their fathers, both the Fathers of the Church and the Fathers of the American Republic. The guardianship of the original American consensus, based on the Western heritage, would have passed to the Catholic community, within which the heritage was elaborated long before America was. And it would be for others, not Catholics, to ask themselves whether they still shared the consensus which first fashioned the American people into a body politic and determined the structure of its fundamental law. [27]

If it be true that this "paradox" has come to pass, that as Murray prophesied Catholics find themselves the party of secular orthodoxy, and that the spiritual children of Pius IX find themselves defending Lockean principles of the civil order, it is unclear by what means this can be expressed in properly political acts. It may well happen, probably sooner than later, that Catholics of good conscience will have to heed the proposition of Martin Luther King, Jr.: "We will use non-cooperation to give birth to justice." [28] Civil disobedience looms not merely as an option, but an obligation. As the black community learned, when the first principles are at issue, there cannot be business as usual. The black community basically said that there will be no civil amity until the injustice is undone.

At least at the political level that we have addressed in this essay, the injustice will be undone when the state no longer recognizes a "fundamental right" to abortion. It is crucial that we be clear why the "right" is the non-negotiable term of the dispute. The answer is that the "right" defines the nature of the political sphere. It is the "right" that must either bind or release political conscience.

To be sure, the official nullification of this "right" will not completely rectify the situation with regard to the unborn. The moral problem of abortion stands at many different levels. The fact that one innocent child is killed, whether by right or toleration, is a moral outrage. But the fact that government recognizes a right to kill the innocent infects the first principles of the civil order. Therefore, unless this is corrected, other moral judgments cannot be brought to bear upon the abortion problem except outside the political sphere. Nor will the nullification of the alleged "right" immediately heal the loss of consensus caused by twenty years of battle over abortion. My point is that it would re-establish the minimum political grounds for reconciling conscience with the regime. Until that happens, it is not so clear that Catholics can have a political home in America.

NOTES

[1] Christopher Dawson, *The Crisis of Western Education* (New York: Sheed and Ward, 1961), p. 97.

[2] John Courtney Murray, *We Hold These Truths: Catholic Reflections on the American Proposition* (New York: Sheed and Ward, 1960).

[3] *Roth v. United States*, 354 U.S. 476 (1957).

[4] *Everson v. Board of Education*, 330 U.S. 1 (1947). For the best history of the way this new jurisprudence departed from the original meaning, see Gerard V. Bradley, *Church-State Relationships in America* (1987).

[5] Which it would do, two years later, in *Engle v. Vitale*, 370 U.S. 421 (1962).

[6] A. James Reichley, *Religion in American Public Life* (Washington, D.C.: Brookings, 1985), p. 145. The percentages were much higher in the South, where seventy-seven percent of the schools required Bible readings. Polls suggested that "secularists" comprised only two percent of the population in 1960. James D. Hunter, *Culture Wars* (New York: Basic Books, 1991), p. 76. "Secularists" are defined as those who respond "none" when questioned about religious preference. Hunter notes, however, that by 1982 this group made up nearly eleven percent of the population, the "fastest growing community of 'moral conviction' in America".

[7] Jacques Maritain, *Reflections on America* (New York: Charles Scribner's Sons, 1958), p. 171.

[8] Ibid., p. 118.

[9] Writing from Princeton during the Second World War, Maritain endorsed the 1929 *International Declaration of the Rights of Man*, which was modeled on section one of the Fourteenth Amendment. Jacques Maritain, *The Rights of Man and Natural Law*, trans. by Doris C. Anson (New York: Gordian Press, 1971 reprint of the 1943 Charles Scribner's edition), p. 115.

[10] Jacques Maritain, *Man and the State* (Chicago: University of Chicago Press, 1951), p. 119.

[11] Ibid., p. 111.

[12] Such a charter would deal, for instance, with the following points: "rights and liberties of the human person, political rights and liberties, social rights and social liberties, corresponding responsibilities; rights and duties of persons who are part of the family society, and liberties and obligations of the latter toward the body politic; mutual rights and duties of groups and the State; government of the people, by the people, and for the people; functions of authority in a political and social democracy; moral obligation, binding in conscience, regarding just laws as well as the Constitution which guarantees the people's liberties. . . ." Ibid., p. 112.

44

[13] William J. Gould, "The Challenge of Liberal Political Culture in the Thought of John Courtney Murray", 19 *Communio* (Spring 1992), p. 139.

[14] Ibid., p. 142.

[15] It was not just Catholic intellectuals who adopted this point of view. Throughout the 1940s and 1950s, European Jewish émigrés, like Leo Strauss, Hannah Arendt, and Jacob Klein, at such institutions as the University of Chicago, the New School, and St. Johns College, emphasized (i) the discontinuity between the American political experiment and the European Enlightenment, and (ii) the continuities between the American experiment and the classical, or pre-modern understanding of the principles of natural justice. In fact, the revival of natural law theory in this country after the Second World War was due primarily to Catholic and to neo-classical Jewish thinkers. Both noted the permeability of the American regime to various philosophical readings. The historical, institutional, and rhetorical presence of natural law in American affairs provided these Catholic and Jewish intellectuals with the ground for developing a "high reading". After all, when Martin Luther King, Jr. issued his famous Letter from Birmingham Jail, he cited as support for the Declaration of Independence St. Augustine and St. Thomas Aquinas. Martin Luther King, Jr., *Why We Can't Wait* (New York: Harper and Row, 1963), pp. 77–100.

[16] *Supra* note 2, p. 182. Dawson clearly indicated his preference for the early, agrarian character of the American Republic. See Christopher Dawson, "America and the Secularization of Modern Culture", The Smith History Lecture of 1960 (Houston: The University of St. Thomas, 1960), pp. 20–21.

[17] Ibid., p. 185.

[18] Ibid.

[19] *Supra*, note 3, p. 41.

[20] For example, concerning John Locke, Murray wrote: "Locke's system was refuted before the system was born"—by Aristotle. *We Hold These Truths*, p. 310. Interestingly, the native-born Murray was more critical of the American mind than were the foreign-born Maritain, Simon, and Dawson.

[21] Of course, things have changed too in the life of the Church. Who could have predicted what happened to the Church, its clergy, and its schools over these past three decades? Who would have predicted that Catholic opinion, in the aggregate percentages, would be virtually indistinguishable from that of the rest of the population on abortion and divorce? Or, as reported in a recent Gallup study of American Catholics, that between 1952 and 1984, Catholics represented the greatest decline of any denomination surveyed in saying that religion is "very important" in their lives? Or, according to the same study, that fewer Catholics hold that premarital sex is wrong than any of the surveyed denominations (only 33% agreed)? George Gallup, Jr. and Jim Castelli, *The American Catholic People* (New York: Doubleday, 1987), pp. 12, 51.

[22] Russell Hittinger, "What Really Happened in the *Casey* Decision", *Crisis* (Sept. 1992), pp. 16–22.

[23] I say "little margin for error" because insofar as government is limited by means of the allocation and enumeration of powers, an oversight or undersight does not necessarily commit the state to a counter-principle. For example, if for some strange reason the founders neglected to grant the government power to prosecute its officers for treasonous acts, this does not mean that anyone has a right to commit treason. It only means that by an oversight, the Framers and ratifiers neglected to give government the power to reach such acts. By analogy, it would be one thing if the Constitutional order gave no organ of the United States government so-called "police powers" over abortion. But it is quite another thing to say that an individual has a right to kill the unborn.

[24] I mean by the "regime", government under the Constitution. Materially speaking, government in this country consists of over 80,000 different entities, from local school boards to dog catchers. David C. Nice, *Federalism: The Politics of Intergovernmental Relations* (1987), p. 2.

[25] If, for some terrible reason, one's wife chose to kill your child, you would have no say in this matter, except at a non-political level. If, again, for some tragic reason, one's daughter elected to kill your grandchild, in many states the law dictates that you will have no say, even when the state itself becomes a party to the act, and even when the daughter is a minor. Since the time of Roman law, this is something approximating the condition of a slave.

[26] Max Farrand, ed., *The Records of the Federal Convention of 1787*, rev. ed. (4 vols.; New Haven, 1937), II, 417.

[27] *Supra*, note 3, pp. 42–43.

[28] Cited in Morton H. Halperin et al., *The Lawless State* (New York: Penguin, 1976), p. 61.

FRANCIS CANAVAN, S.J.

POLITICAL CHOICE
AND CATHOLIC CONSCIENCE

"*Politique d'abord*—politics first of all!" was the slogan of Charles Maurras, an avowed atheist and French ultra-nationalist in the first half of this century. That slogan is almost unknown in this country, but it is the unspoken assumption of millions of Americans, including a number of Catholic politicians who don't speak a word of French and never heard of Charles Maurras. When it comes to the crunch, however, they regularly subordinate the dictates of Catholic conscience to the demand of politics.

On the other hand, one cannot say—and I certainly do not mean to imply—that the Catholic conscience requires that all of its dictates be translated into civil and criminal law. In Catholic thought, the relationship between conscience and political decision-making is considerably more nuanced than that.

Let me begin with the view on this subject of Francisco Suarez, S.J., in his great treatise, *De legibus (On Laws)*. Suarez was not the greatest or most authoritative theologian who ever lived, but I choose him for three reasons. One is that I have read Suarez, and there are many and possibly better theologians whom I have not read. Besides, he died one year after William Shakespeare, and so clearly is not a wild-eyed post-Vatican II radical. Finally, and most importantly, he expounds an understanding of the nature and goals of the state that can be traced back to St. Thomas Aquinas.

Prior to Aquinas, the common opinion of the Fathers of the Church was that the state and its coercive power are consequences of original sin. Had the original Paradise lasted, the state would not have been necessary, because men would have behaved morally without needing laws and criminal sanctions. Aquinas took over Aristotle's thesis that man is by nature a social animal and that the state (the *polis* in Aristotle's terminology) is a necessary consequence of man's social nature. In Thomistic theory, the state is not a mere repressor of evil, and its authority does not consist solely in its power to coerce. The state would have been necessary even among uncorrupted and wholly good people, because even they, too, could disagree about the best ways to achieve good ends. They would therefore need authority as a directive principle guiding them toward the goals of the community. For St. Thomas, therefore, the state is a natural community, without which a fully human life is not possible, and its authority is a natural human good.

One can say that Aquinas brought the idea of the state into medieval Catholic thought. Slowly, ever so slowly, this idea shifted the focus of discussion from the relationship of the temporal and spiritual jurisdictions within a single, unified *res publica Christiana* to the relationship between the state and the Church. Even Suarez, who inherited the Thomistic notion of the state as a natural entity and who wrote five hundred and more years after Aquinas, had not yet fully broken away from the *res publica Christiana* and the subordination of the state to the Church—but that is not my reason for citing him here.

According to Suarez, the state is an institution of the natural order, and is not of its nature directed to man's supernatural and eternal end, but only to his temporal happiness, his welfare in this life. Even in this life, the state does not per se look to the spiritual welfare of men, and consequently the state cannot make laws disposing of or regulating spiritual matters— those are the domain of the Church. Nor is even the natural welfare of individual men as individuals the proper end of the state. The natural and proper function of the state is to provide for the secular well-being of the civil community, that is to say, for its temporal common good. The welfare of individuals concerns the state only insofar as they are members of that community.[1]

As the goal of the state and its government is limited to the temporal common good of the political community, so is its power to make laws. So also, therefore, is the area of political decision-making limited. That, therefore, is the arena in which the Catholic conscience, like the conscience of any other group of citizens, has its proper field of operation. The Catholic conscience looks to the state and its lawmaking power to legislate morality only insofar as a public morality is a component element of the temporal common good of the whole community.

This is the position that the Second Vatican Council took in its Declaration on Religious Freedom. "The common welfare of society", it said, "consists in the entirety of those conditions of social life under which men enjoy the possibility of achieving their own perfection in a certain fullness of measure and also with some relative ease."[2] According to the Council, it is up to men to achieve their own perfection, that is, their physical, mental, and spiritual development. The role of the state is to promote those conditions of social life that facilitate, and do not impede, that development. The main thrust of the Declaration is that among those conditions is religious freedom.

In promoting the common good, therefore, the Declaration explains:

> Government is not to act in an arbitrary fashion or in an unfair spirit of partisanship. Its action is to be controlled by juridical norms which are in conformity with the objective moral order. These norms arise out of the need for effective safeguard of the rights of all citizens and for peaceful settlement of conflicts of rights. They flow from the need for an adequate care of genuine public peace, which comes about when men live together in good order and in true justice. They come finally, out of the need for a proper guardianship of public morality. These matters constitute the basic component of the common welfare; they are what is meant by public order.

For the rest, the usages of society are to be the usages of freedom in their full range.[3] We can thus say that Vatican II supported the principle of limited government, but that it recognized a common social good and an objective moral order to which the state's juridical norms should conform. In this it was in harmony with the American legal tradition. The Preamble to the U.S. Constitution states the purposes for which the American people have framed their Constitution: "We the People of the United States, in Order to form a more perfect Union, establish Justice, insure domestic Tranquility, provide for the common defense, promote the general Welfare, and secure the Blessings of Liberty to ourselves and our Posterity, do ordain and establish this Constitution for the United States of America." Justice is surely a moral concept and, along with domestic tranquility, common defense, general welfare, and liberty, it is an element of the common good of the United States.

Broad as those terms are, however, they state the purpose of a federal constitution, which establishes a national government with limited powers, and assumes the existence of the several States of the Union, with their own powers derived from their State citizens. Among these State powers is what is called the police power. Various State courts over the years have defined this power as "the function of that branch of the administrative machinery of government which is charged with the preservation of public order and tranquility, the promotion of the public health, safety, and morals, and the prevention, detection, and punishment of crimes", and as "the power vested in the legislature to make, ordain, and establish all manner of wholesome and reasonable laws, statutes, and ordinances, either with penalties or without, not repugnant to the constitution, as they shall judge to be for the good and welfare of the commonwealth, and of the subjects of the same."[4] These definitions assume that, within the limits set by the State and Federal constitutions, State governments are empowered to legislate and administer for the public health, safety, welfare, and morals.

If governments may act for these ends, it must be possible for the people to discuss and debate both the ends and the means to them, and to arrive at decisions in public law and policy to effectuate them, through the procedures of democratic politics. But this proposition is more and more called into question by the radically individualistic and secularist view which has become the liberal orthodoxy of the opinion-making sectors of this country. One of the more extreme examples of this orthodoxy is H. Tristam Engelhardt's *The Foundations of Bioethics*,[5] in which he argues that there is no substantive moral standard of any kind which can be the basis of a public morality in a pluralistic society, because there is no such standard to which all members of the society can agree on either religious or rational grounds. The only possible basis for our common life in American society, he says, is a set of procedures to which all of us can agree as the necessary condition of our living together in peace. Those procedures become a binding moral commitment for each of us, precisely because we have agreed to them: "The moral world can be fashioned through free will, even if not on the basis of sound rational arguments with moral content."[6]

But then it turns out that there are necessary exceptions to what we can agree to. Even if we have agreed, for example, to make decisions by majority vote, some issues may not be decided by majority, not even by majorities of two-thirds or three-fourths, "unless *all* can be presumed to have agreed in advance to such procedures". But that is to say that there are substantive exceptions to the procedures:

> One might think here of individuals wishing to acquire contraceptives, have abortions, take hallucinogens, or end their own lives. Laws forbidding such, even if enacted by a majority of three-fourths of the populace, are not simply of dubious authority, but may properly be seen to be attempts to use unconsented-to force against the innocent.[7]

On those terms, however, why are there any limits to the exceptions that must be made, if not only the procedures but their results must have universal consent? One might think here of individuals wishing to acquire several wives or husbands at the same time, have sexual relations with pubescent adolescents (who are supposed to be old enough to have abortions without notifying their parents), to engage in sado-masochism, or to practice ritual human sacrifice with willing victims, if such can be found. Or why is smoking cigarettes in public not included in the list of things that not everyone has consented to ban? One might also want to discuss whether abortion is not a use of unconsented-to force against the innocent, and why that is taken to be a closed question that may not legitimately be raised in a pluralistic society.

But let that pass. The point to be emphasized here is that every such effort to persuade us to accept a purely procedural and substantively neutral model of civil society, in which no particular notion of human good is permitted to prevail at the public level, is a flim-flam and a confidence game. It is designed to lure us into agreeing to a highly individualistic and secularist liberal agenda which has its own substantive content.[8] For there is no such thing as a society which is simply neutral on all questions of substantive human good. Yet those questions are what we mean by moral issues.

It does not follow that all questions of human good and morality belong in the public domain. All non-totalitarian societies draw a line between private and public moral issues, a boundary between those areas of life which are left to private choice and those that are subject to public regulation. But where that line should be drawn is itself a matter for public decision because, to safeguard the realm of private decision, there must be laws that define and protect it.

Furthermore, the public decision to protect areas of conduct regarded as private can and does vary with time and circumstance. In New York today people may legally appear naked on the stage, but the people in the audience may not smoke while looking at them. There was a time within living memory when the reverse was true. Drawing the line therefore is a political issue and one that inevitably will often have to be argued in moral terms.

To hold otherwise would be to give every group and even every individual the power to veto any public policy that embodies some conception of what human beings are and what is good for them. It would therefore constantly subordinate any understanding of the common good of society to the will of dissenters. In saying this I am not proposing a Catholic, Christian, Judeo-Christian, or any other religious orthodoxy for the pluralistic society of this country. I am only saying that political issues at some point or other raise moral questions that must be answered in the light of some conception of human nature, its basic needs, and its common social welfare. If there is nothing we can agree on about human good, then we cannot act for the welfare of our community.

If we have a welfare state, do we not need to come to some agreement on what we mean by welfare? If we take the family as an object of public policy because of its importance to society, do we not have to define the family and decide what helps or hinders it? If we wish to promote public health, must we not decide whether it ranks above or below sexual gratification, the issue which is just below the surface in the current controversy over how to respond to the spread of AIDS? These and a host of other questions are ones that even a pluralistic society must answer, and it cannot answer them all by leaving them to private consciences.

A country's laws and public policies necessarily reflect the conscience of the people, either of the people as a whole or of the dominant element among them. In a society like ours, which is becoming steadily more pluralistic, the common conscience is shrinking or even crumbling, and public decisions based on it are becoming more difficult to arrive at. Yet decisions must be arrived at. They cannot all be left to the individual and his private choice, because so many of them involve a view, not only of what is good for the individual, but of what is good for the community of which he is a part.

Whatever may be the grimy reality of politics, it is in principle a process by which a community comes to decisions about action for its common good. Sometimes, however, it is feared that the issues thus raised are too explosive for the political process to handle. The U.S. Supreme Court has occasionally tried to take explosively divisive issues out of the political process, most notably in *Dred Scott v. Sandford* in 1857 and *Roe v. Wade* in 1973. Such efforts often fail, however, because they do not resolve the issue in a way that both sides can accept, however reluctantly, but simply decree the victory of one side over the other. Deeply divisive issues are seldom fully resolved, but they can be brought to partial resolutions through the normal political process, and the Court would be wise to let it function. The battle over the issues will continue, but it will be a legal and nonviolent political contest in which people can learn to live with the temporary results, while hoping to achieve better ones at a later date.

Politics in a secular democratic state is concerned with the content of the temporal good of the community in this world, and with the means of achieving it. Both the content and the means are subject to political dispute and debate. It does not follow that only secularists may take part in the debate, or that Catholics must check their consciences at the door when entering the public forum, or that we must obey the secularists when they shout: "Sit down, shut up, and let us run the country!" Catholics, like all other citizens, have a right to bring their view of the public welfare, informed by their conscience, to bear on questions that are properly issues of public policy. The state is separate from the church, but it is not separate from the consciences that churches form.

A recent example of secularist arrogance appeared, not in the *New York Times*, where you might expect it, but in an editorial in the *San Antonio [Texas] Express-News* on August 30, 1992: "This nation's goodness is deep-rooted and only superficially religion-based." That statement is in itself a very superficial judgment. It is true, and zealots should never forget it, that we can seldom argue directly from religious premises to concrete public-policy conclusions as if those conclusions were the manifest will of God. But it is equally naïve to ignore the social reality that a people's laws reflect their moral convictions, that these in turn reflect their beliefs about the nature of man and of the world we live in, and that such beliefs historically have been rooted in their religion or religions. It is worth mentioning that the religions of this country, despite their multiplicity, have generally shared a common Biblical moral tradition.

A universe created by a personal and loving God, and populated by persons made in the image and likeness of God is a vastly different place from a universe that has evolved through the blind operation of the forces of matter, and is populated by humanoids who, far from being a little less than the angels (for there are no angels), are only a cut above the apes. Whichever of these two views you hold will not tell you whether we should or should not reduce the capital gains tax. But it will have a profound effect on how you think about deeper and much more important issues.

James Fitzjames Stephen saw this clearly in England as long ago as 1873. Stephen lost his faith in Christianity altogether, but he nonetheless said that if belief in a personal God and a future life should disappear, "there will be an end of what is commonly called religion, and it will be necessary to reconstruct morals from end to end".[9] The reason he gave was this:

> If these beliefs are mere dreams, life is a very much poorer and pettier thing; men are beings of much less importance; trouble, danger, and physical pain are much greater evils, and the prudence of virtue is much more questionable than has hitherto been supposed to be the case. If men follow the advice so often pressed upon them, to cease to think of these subjects otherwise than as insoluble riddles, all the existing conceptions of morality will have to be changed, all social tendencies will be weakened. Merely personal inclinations will be greatly strengthened.[10]

In particular, said Stephen, "The value which is set upon human life, especially upon the lives of the sick, the wretched, and superfluous children would at once appear to be exaggerated. Lawyers would have occasion to reconsider the law of murder, and especially the law of infanticide."[11]

We have reached that point today, and we must give Stephen credit for having foreseen, well over a century ago, what so many people who call themselves Christians and Catholics refuse to see at this late date.

It is, of course, irrelevant, although secularists will rush to remind us of it, that some Catholics are worse in their personal lives than highminded agnostics. It is also a sublime missing of the point to say that we live in a pluralistic society and must therefore settle for the lowest common denominator in our public morality. *The lowest denominator is not common.* To take the most obvious examples, we do not all hold a secularist view of the value of human life, of the meaning and importance of sex, and of the nature of marriage and the family. It is begging the question to assume that because we disagree on them, therefore these are all subjects of merely personal choice, of little or no significance to society and its common good.

On the contrary, these matters are properly in the public forum and are subject to public debate and possible regulation. A Catholic understanding of them has as much right as any other to present itself and to influence public decisions concerning them. I do not say that Catholics have a right to force others to accept their faith. Nor do I suggest that sound public policies in regard to these matters depend on a general acceptance of Catholic theology. I do say that Catholics may and should vigorously present their understanding of these and other topics of vital concern to the whole community's general welfare.

If we do that, without allowing ourselves to be brow-beaten into silence, we may reasonably hope to find areas of agreement with many of our fellow citizens who are not of our faith, and even with some who have no religious faith. After all, there are agnostics and atheists who feel that 1-1/2 million abortions a year are too many, that easy divorce has seriously undesirable social effects, that the sexual preachments of Madonna and other heralds of the new morality do not furnish a sound basis for public education, and that homosexuality is not really on a par with heterosexuality when we legislate concerning marriage.

At this point, I should proceed to make some important distinctions about what Catholics (or any other group) should try to accomplish through political and legal action. As Edmund Burke put it, it is no inconsiderable part of wisdom to know how much of an evil ought to be tolerated. But, precisely because it requires so much practical, prudential wisdom to know when and how to act against evils, and when to refrain from action, discussing this aspect of the subject would take more time and space than I have at my present disposal. I shall merely note that a full discussion of political choice and Catholic conscience would require taking up that topic, and let it rest there. My main, and indeed only, point has been that while the authority of the state is limited to the secular, temporal good of the civil community, even in that area politics is not supreme and a law unto itself. It is subject to the moral judgment of the citizens, including those who believe in the God in whom this nation allegedly trusts.

NOTES

[1] For Suarez's own words, see the footnotes in an article, "Subordination of the State to the Church in Suarez", that I had published in *Theological Studies* 12 (1951): pp. 354–364.

[2] Declaration on Religious Freedom, Sect. 6, *The Documents of Vatican II*, ed. Abbott and Gallagher (New York: Guild Press, America Press, Association Press, 1966), p. 683.

[3] Ibid., Sect. 7, pp. 686–87.

[4] *Black's Law Dictionary* (St. Paul, Minn.: West Publishing Co., 1951). p. 1316, col. 1, and p. 1317, col. 1.

[5] H. Tristam Engelhardt, *The Foundations of Bioethics* (New York and Oxford: Oxford University Press, 1986).

[6] Ibid., p. 42.

[7] Ibid., p. 46.

[8] I have developed this theme at length in "The Pluralist Game", *Law and Contemporary Problems* 44 (1981): pp. 23–37.

[9] James Fitzjames Stephen, *Liberty, Equality, Fraternity* (reprinted by the Cambridge University Press in 1967), p. 39.

[10] Ibid., p. 98.

[11] Ibid., p. 48.

WILLIAM BENTLEY BALL

THE EFFECT OF CURRENT JUDICIAL DECISIONS ON THE PLACE OF CATHOLICS IN THE LIFE OF THE COUNTRY

The topic I am asked to address involves three questions: (1) Who are the Catholics who will be affected by the judicial decisions in question?[1] (2) Who are those who are rendering those judicial decisions? (3) What is the import of those decisions?

Catholics

In answering my first question, I was about to speak of "the Catholics". But that would have been a carry-over from days when there was a clearly identifiable collectivity to whom the Catholic Faith, as taught under infallible guidance, was the one true Faith, and to whom that Faith was the most important thing in their lives. Today it is oddly not seen by Church leaders that there will be no real Catholic community again until those who label themselves "Catholic" embrace the Faith with the ardent fidelity with which it was embraced by Catholics in this country prior to Vatican II.

Therefore, when we speak of the effect today of judicial decisions in the United States upon "Catholics" we are put to distinguishing three groups of those who bear the "Catholic" label. The first of these are those Catholics having the fidelity and allegiance that I have just described (and whom I call "orthodox" Catholics). They weigh major judicial decisions precisely in terms of traditional Catholic concepts of morality and justice. As we shall see, this may plunge them into public controversy, cause them intense pain or rejoicing, motivate them to be actors on great issues, be it neighbor-to-neighbor, or in the courts, legislatures, or the media. The second group are those who seek to blend into the morally featureless landscape of the general populace. They (in great numbers, it seems) are untroubled by the court decisions which so stir the orthodox. They not only see nothing to warrant excitement over these; they are indeed often annoyed and embarrassed by what they deem the "overreacting" of the orthodox. This bland mentality is notably present among affluent Catholics, comfortable, financially contributing church-goers, eager in this generation to enjoy social status and to avoid the taint of looking "different". Third are those who bear the label "Catholic" and who support judicial decisions attacking Catholic principles of morality and justice. Precisely because of their identification with the Church whose teachings they repudiate, they lend at once enormous strength to the forces which impel us toward chaos and, by their example, publicize a message to all Catholics and to the world that the Church is wrong in its teachings. The effect on them of the unjust or morally bad decisions of the courts is important, since those decisions will trigger these nominal Catholics to publicly confirm the evils of the decisions. These differences among Catholics being noted, I will consider only the first group, the "orthodox", in discussing our problem of the effect of court decisions.

Judges

I come now to my second question: who are those who are rendering the judicial decisions affecting (or not affecting, or affecting in different ways) Catholics?

Over a period of several decades I have been standing before judges. I have seen, among them, men and women virtuous, corrupt, learned, ignorant, rude saints and courteous scamps.

But it is at that high peak of all our courts—the one we call "Supreme"—that I have focused especially on the quality of judges. I mean by that three things: character, learning, and capacity to judge. Judge what, at the Supreme Court level? The gravest, most profound, and intractable problems facing this vast people of ours. What presumption it would seem that any person might deem himself fit to accept a call to sit in judgment upon such issues! And with the knowledge that he or she alone, in the case of a 5–4 decision of that Court, might be deciding issues of life and death, liberty or oppression, good or evil for 250 million other citizens.

How do we find these three characteristics which we need in judges? Character presents a difficult problem because honorableness is so readily at war, in many natures, with the appetite for honors. The desire to be well regarded in circles of prestige and power I count as a far more significant temptation among justices of the Supreme Court than the bribes of money or political favor which are often the temptations at lower court levels. It is a sad commentary on our times, but a reflection of the oldest of problems, that gaining a line of commendation from the New York Times or being praised by major media for "growth" in "judicial statesmanship" may prove an irresistible temptation to those who sit on the High Court.

I am at a loss to know what to do to assure character in our justices. Screening of candidates will likely serve to reveal prior corruption but will be far less likely to disclose the poisonous root of vanity hidden in the dark and inaccessible recesses of the psyche.

What about the second needed characteristic—learning? Most of our justices have had little but law-book learning. The American law schools of today no longer draw on the wellsprings of ancient learning in the law. If you compare opinions of most of the justices today with those of the great jurists of a century and a half—or even a century—ago (I think of Kent or Story), the diminution in learning and in quality of expression, is startling. Partly the difference is due to ignorance that problems the Court faces today were already experienced, pondered, and dealt with centuries before. But justices who are as ignorant of the classical learning found in literature of the past as they are of history—people like the late Justice Hugo Black, a political creature who rose to exercise the great power of a Supreme Court justiceship from a career which was nothing but the story of a political hack—will not only fail to benefit from lessons of history but will—as did Black—write bad history borrowed from people he regarded as his intellectual superiors.

It is not surprising, then, that we get some opinions from the High Court which are, at worst, unreadable or at best, the kind of banal attempts at noble expression which political speech writers purvey.

Our third criterion is the capacity to judge. Not in order to please Drs. Benestad and Hittinger, who are with us today, but to state a stark truth, I will venture that justices who are untrained in the scholastic principles of reasoning cannot be relied upon to judge well. In some decisions of the Supreme Court—notably in reference to abortion—we are being paved over with non-sequiturs, missing premises, imponderable language, failure to know that a thing cannot at the same time be true and not true.

I do not mean to say that the Supreme Court today is dominated by people of poor character, ignorance, or incapacity to judge. It is instead a quite mixed picture. But I feel that, in the matter of judicial selection, the predominance of political factors (as in the shocking case of Robert Bork) are not more significant than the failure to bring into sharp focus the three criteria I have described. We must face it, however, that our courts and our Supreme Court are not likely to rise higher than the quality of the culture from which their judges are derived. Learning is on the decline in our nation and indeed political correctness is now suffocating real intellectuality. Along with this goes the vanishing of philosophy. But most of all, a society without virtue cannot beget governors—and judges—of virtue.[2]

The Decisions

Article VI of the American Constitution states: "This Constitution . . . shall be the supreme Law of the Land." But the oldest debate in our constitutional law concerns, not whether the Constitution is supreme but whether, or in what sense, the Supreme Court is. Lincoln once said:

> . . . if the policy of the Government upon vital questions affecting the whole people is to be irrevocably fixed by decisions of the Supreme Court, the instant they are made in ordinary litigation between parties in personal actions, the people will have ceased to be their own rulers, having to that extent practically resigned their government into the hands of that eminent tribunal.[3]

For many decades, however, we have largely resigned our governance into the hands of that Court. This fact underscores our inquiry concerning the effect of its decisions on the place of Catholics in the life of our country. Catholics are not singularly affected by most decisions of the Court. When the Supreme Court hands down rulings in the fields of fair trade, the environment, taxation, labor relations, shipping, and myriad other areas, Catholics, if affected at all, are usually affected commonly with everybody else. But there are at least three areas of Supreme Court decisions which have affected Catholics either solely or along with only a small number of other citizens. These areas we can loosely identify as:

> Education Questions
> Questions of Catholic Citizenship
> Right-to-Life Questions

1. *Education Questions.* The question of whether parents who choose to enroll their children in Catholic schools may be aided by tax funds to do it has been with us since the 1840s. Then, and throughout the nineteenth century, the question was so shrouded in anti-Catholic denunciation that it could scarcely be recognized for what it was—simply an issue of whether

citizens who choose to obtain education in non-governmental schools should be barred—solely on religious grounds—from participation in tax benefits equal to those awarded citizens who choose the government schools. The injustice was long worsened by the fact that, well into the twentieth century, many government schools were strongly Protestant in their orientation. The specific hatred of the Catholic school was soon embodied in the pre-Civil War "anti-aid" amendment to the Massachusetts Constitution,[4] and, after the Civil War, in the Blaine Amendments lodged in most State constitutions. This was logical in a society in which the majority of the highly educated had absorbed their knowledge of the Catholic Church from the histories of Gibbon, Macaulay, Motley, and Prescott and, above all, from ministers in their churches.

What effect did this pointed exclusion have upon Catholics? Undoubtedly it contributed to their militancy in building their schools, seeking to protect those schools from dangerous state regulation, and in continuing to press for public aid. So it was, that the central role of the Catholic school in the consciousness of Catholic citizens continued until shortly after the Second Vatican Council. They continued to press, with fervor, the "aid" question in the assemblies of many states. Until 1947 the Supreme Court had had occasion to touch upon constitutional aspects of that question only three times—these being in cases where relevance to the "aid" issue was now marginal, either because the decisions were far in the past or because they were not precisely in point.[5] The major decision of the Supreme Court in 1947, in the case of *Everson v. Board of Education*,[6] however, brought the Catholic school explicitly to the fore as the centerpiece of a constitutional litigation. The case involved the public's reimbursing of parents of children enrolled in Catholic schools for the costs of transporting them by the public bus transportation system. Justice Black, for a 5–4 majority, upheld the program against an Establishment Clause attack. His opinion did not center on the schools, other than by identifying them as schools which provided both religious and secular education and which met the secular education requirements which the state was empowered to impose. He upheld the reimbursement as aid, not to the schools but to the children attending them (and to their parents). Justice Robert H. Jackson, of Nuremberg trial fame, in a dissenting opinion which we shall later more fully examine, said that the most fitting precedent for Black's opinion was that of Lord Byron's Julia who, according to Byron's report, "whispering 'I will ne'er consent,'—consented". That was because Jackson believed the Court's decision flew in the face of what its opinion had said about the Establishment Clause. It is that part of the Black opinion which revolutionized interpretation of the religion provisions of the First Amendment. Black said that the Amendment's Establishment Clause created a wall of separation between church and state and that "[n]o tax in any amount, large or small, can be levied to support any religious activity or institution. . . ." Black thus provided the pretext (amply contradicted by history[7]) for the voiding, in the future, of most meaningful legislation supportive of the parental choice of religious schools.

Thus, while in *Board of Education v. Allen*,[8] in 1968, the Court upheld loans of secular textbooks to nonpublic (including religious) school children, it voided more meaningful aid in *Lemon v. Kurtzman* (1971),[9] *Committee For Public Education v. Nyquist* (1973),[10] *Meek v. Pittenger* (1975),[11] *Grand Rapids School District v. Ball* (1985),[12] and *Aguilar v. Felton* (1985).[13] These decisions were the progeny of the Establishment Clause doctrine of *Everson*. What effect have they had on Catholics in our society?

Two effects of these decisions upon Catholics can be seen over the forty-five-year span between 1947 and today. The first, at its most intense between 1947 and 1975, was a renewed zeal by Catholics to obtain public aid for Catholic schools (or the parents enrolling their children there). Major "aid" bills were pressed for by Catholic lobbies in a dozen states. In every instance ACLU, American Jewish Congress, and various public school coalitions brought these into litigation, and we have noted the flow of adverse decisions in these cases.

But in the mid-1960s appeared a sentiment quite to the contrary of the so-called "parochiaid" sentiment. It originated among Catholic college leaders and, though partly a reaction of undue respect for the aggressive tactics of ACLU, AJC, and other church-state separation extremists, was essentially a reaction of so-called "progressivism" within the Church in America. The Fordham Study, in the late 1960s, urged that the colleges (and by implication) the schools, seek public aid as secular institutions. If religious character was the reason why the Constitution could be employed to bar aid, the simple answer was to be rid of vital aspects of the religious character. The authors of the study and the enthusiasts who promoted it gave abundant assurances that this was not their intention at all. They said that the institutions would still be "Catholic" despite certain major alterations in their lives. The whole scheme was brought to fruition in the 1971 case of *Tilton v. Richardson*.[14] In that case four Catholic colleges in Connecticut had received federal construction grants under the Higher Education Facilities Act of 1963. In a suit brought by Leo Pfeffer, this aid was challenged as violating the Establishment Clause. With the aid and endorsement of the United States Catholic Conference, the noted attorney Edward Bennett Williams was retained for the colleges and was provided a trial scenario to follow in conducting the defense of the grants. The scenario was based on the Fordham Study principles. Williams, faithful to the scenario, built a record which showed the following (I quote now from the Supreme Court's opinion in the case):

> The institutions presented evidence that there had been no religious services or worship in the federally financed facilities, that there had been no religious symbols or plaques in or on them . . . [t]hese buildings are indistinguishable from a typical state university facility.
>
> There is no evidence that religion seeps into the use of any of these facilities. Indeed, the parties stipulated . . . that courses

at these institutions are taught according to the academic requirements intrinsic to the subject matter and the individual teacher's concept of professional standards. Although appellants introduced several institutional documents which stated certain religious restrictions on what could be taught, other evidence showed that these restrictions were not in fact enforced and that the schools were characterized by an atmosphere of academic freedom rather than religious indoctrination. All four institutions, for example, subscribe to the 1940 Statement of Principles on Academic Freedom and Tenure endorsed by the American Association of University Professors and the Association of American Colleges.

Not one of these four institutions requires its students to attend religious services. Although all four schools require their students to take theology courses, the parties stipulated that these courses are taught according to the academic requirements of the subject matter and the teacher's concept of professional standards. The parties also stipulated that the courses covered a range of human religious experiences and are not limited to courses about the Roman Catholic religion. The schools introduced evidence that they made no attempt to indoctrinate students or to proselytize. Indeed, some of the required theology courses at Albertus Magnus and Sacred Heart are taught by rabbis.[15]

The *Tilton* decision was followed in 1976 by *Roemer v. Board of Public Works*,[16] involving aid by the state of Maryland, in the form of money grants to religious colleges. Among these colleges were Mount St. Mary's, St. Joseph, Loyola, and College of Notre Dame. Upholding the grants against the Establishment Clause challenge, the Court reviewed the character of the colleges in question. Of these it said:

Though controlled and largely populated by Roman Catholics, the colleges were not restricted to adherents of that faith. No religious services were required to be attended. Theology courses were mandatory, but they were taught in an academic fashion, and with treatment of beliefs other than Roman Catholicism. There were no attempts to proselytize among students, and principles of academic freedom prevailed. With colleges of this character, there was little risk that religion would seep into the teaching of secular subjects, and the state surveillance necessary to separate the two, therefore, was diminished.[17]

In addition:

Despite their formal affiliation with the Roman Catholic Church, the colleges are "characterized by a high degree of institutional autonomy." . . . None of the four receives funds from, or makes reports to, the Catholic Church. The Church is represented on their governing boards, but, as with Mount Saint Mary's, "no instance of entry of Church considerations into college decisions was shown."

The colleges employ Roman Catholic chaplains and hold Roman Catholic religious exercises on campus. Attendance at such is not required; the encouragement of spiritual development is only "one secondary objective" of each college; and "at none of these institutions does this encouragement go beyond providing the opportunities or occasions for religious experiences."

Some classes are begun with prayer. The percentage of classes in which this is done varies with the college, from a "minuscule" percentage at Loyola and Mount Saint Mary's, to a majority at Saint Joseph. . . . There is no "actual college policy" of encouraging the practice.[18]

What effect did these decisions have on Catholics? Doubtless a considerable effect since they added a powerful argument to the stance taken by "progressive" Catholic college leaders against rights asserted by bishops respecting the duties of Catholic institutions. The colleges could now argue that the very existence of Catholic higher education depended on government aid and that government aid was barred to institutions which insisted upon maintaining a full, permeant religious character. A second, broader, effect conceivably flowed from the first effect: the popularization of the two-faced Catholic college—the secular face shown to government, to prestigious persons, and accrediting bodies in secular academia, and the religious face shown to bishops and to the market of those Catholic parents who "want my kid to get a real Catholic education", many of whom would now reap disappointment since the real thing would not be available to the kid and, in the new religiously free-wheeling environment, he might indeed conclude that the Faith was irrelevant to his life.

Did these decisions on governmental aid have any effect upon Catholics in respect to their elementary and secondary schools? Since 1970 the schools have of course experienced a great decline in attendance and in religious as faculty members. That was due only marginally to economic conditions. In the Catholic past, as with the orthodox Evangelical present, religious schools *will* be founded and maintained by people to whom their religion is absolutely true and to whom that religion is the most important thing in their lives. The years following Vatican II saw a widespread decline of faith among Catholics. The negative school aid decisions and the popularity of secularizing the colleges, however, had indeed some effects on the Catholic grade and high schools. That effect consisted of a defensiveness, a hunger for a new image and an unwarranted truckling to public school standard-setters in order to achieve that image. "Excellence" and "relevance" became slogans by which too many Catholic school administrators were able to justify subservience to burdensome, needless, and sometimes incomprehensible or unconstitutional regulations by State education boards or departments.[19] In a few states today—notably Pennsylvania—Catholic educators have taken a good cue from Evangelical educators and joined them in successfully resisting improper state regulations.[20]

2. *The Question of Catholic Citizenship.* Let me now return to 1947 and the *Everson* case. There were four justices in that case who vigorously dissented, not from Justice Black's absolutist interpretation of the Establishment Clause, but from his allowance that public payment for busing of parochial school children did not fall on the outer side of the wall of church-state separation to which he had referred. These justices, in their dissent, made the *Catholic* nature and Church governance of Catholic schools the hot focal point of their denunciation

of the decision. Justice Jackson said that whether the parents or children could be aided by state paid-for busing "depends upon the nature of those [Catholic] schools and their relating to the Church".[21] He then turned to the Code of Canon Law of the Church and there found that indeed the Code required the schools to be Catholic, that bishops had ultimate power over them to insure doctrinal fidelity, and that "Catholic children shall not attend non-Catholic, indifferent schools that are mixed, that is to say, open to Catholics and non-Catholics alike." He opined that it was "no exaggeration to say that the whole historic conflict between the Catholic Church and non-Catholics comes to a focus in their respective school policies". He said that "[o]ur public school, if not a product of Protestantism, at least is more consistent with it than with the Catholic culture and scheme of values."[22]

It is sad today to reflect upon Jackson's estimation of Catholic education as of 1947:

> I should be surprised if any Catholic would deny that the parochial school is a vital, if not the most vital, part of the Roman Catholic Church. If put to the choice, that venerable institution, I should expect, would forego its whole service for mature persons before it would give up education of the young, and it would be a wise choice. Its growth and cohesion, discipline and loyalty, spring from its schools. Catholic education is the rock on which the whole structure rests, and to render tax aid to its Church school is distinguishable to me from rendering the same aid to the Church itself.[23]

In this tribute and the preceding statements of Jackson which I have quoted is an identification of the Catholic as someone whose citizenship, respectfully, is necessarily suspect. The children of the "venerable institution's" members may not be accorded busing at public cost, albeit, at least in 1947, children in public schools (which still reflected a Protestant ethos) could be afforded that form of aid.

A far more explicit statement on the citizenship of Catholics came about in 1971, in the now famous case of *Lemon v. Kurtzman.*[24] Lemon involved programs of state aid to non-public (including religious) schools. The Court invalidated the programs on the ground that they violated the Establishment Clause of the First Amendment. This invalidation was based on new, home-made law: the notion that the Establishment Clause bars relationships between government and religious entities which would call for "excessive entanglements" between the two. Quite correctly, the Court did not cite as authority a single one of the drafters of the Constitution, or indeed any source prior to 1969. No such authority existed. It instead relied for its authority on an article by Professor Paul Freund from *Harvard Law Review*[25] which appeared in 1969—and which itself cited no statement by any of the Framers of the Constitution upon which it could rely. A key point in Freund's article concerned political entanglements:

> Ordinarily political debate and division, however vigorous or even partisan, are normal and healthful manifestations of our democratic system of government, but political division along religious lines was one of the principal evils against which the First Amendment was intended to protect. . . . The potential divisiveness of such conflict is a threat to the normal political process.[26]

This doctrine had been unheard of. American history is filled with examples of "political division along religious lines". Abolitionism, Prohibition, the 1960s civil rights and peace movements, and campaigns for aid to Israel are but the most obvious examples. But the Court went on with the Freund notion:

> To have States or communities divide on the issues presented by state aid to parochial schools would tend to confuse and obscure other issues of great urgency. We have an expanding array of vexing issues, local and national, domestic and international, to debate and divide on. It conflicts with our whole history and tradition to permit questions of the Religion Clauses to assume such importance in our legislatures and in our elections that they could divert attention from the myriad issues and problems which confront every level of government.[27]

"*To have* States or communities" divide on the parochial school aid issue means, of course, "For the Court to *permit*" such division. What the people choose through the democratic processes must be denied them since those processes are contaminated by arguments—*arguments* over religion.

The Court then sought to absolve itself of appearing suppressive:

> Of course, as the Court noted in *Walz,* "adherents of particular faiths and individual churches frequently take strong positions on public issues." . . . We could not expect otherwise, for religious values pervade the fabric of our national life.[28]

But it then pulled the rug out from under its own specious pretension and now got down to whom it was really talking about:

> Here we are confronted with successive and very likely permanent annual appropriations which benefit relatively few religious groups. Political fragmentation and divisiveness on religious lines is thus likely to be intensified.
>
> The potential for political divisiveness related to religious belief and practice is aggravated in these two statutory programs by the need for continuing annual appropriations and the likelihood of larger and larger demands as costs and populations grow.[29]

Of course it was speaking of Catholic citizens and the Catholic Church. As everyone knew, it was they who had originated the Rhode Island and Pennsylvania statutes in question and campaigned for them.

Such was the *Lemon* Court's first conclusion respecting the citizenship of Catholics. That is, their political activity must be frustrated. A second conclusion concerned the personal integrity of Catholic citizens who teach in the Catholic schools. The Pennsylvania statute invalidated in *Lemon* called for state purchase of service in courses in mathematics, physical science, physical education, and modern foreign languages—subjects not readily lent to religious infusion. And the statute prohibited such infusions. But the Supreme Court flatly held that a teacher in a Catholic school was not to be trusted to observe the law:

> The teacher is employed by a religious organization, subject to the direction and discipline of religious authorities, and works in a system dedicated to rearing children in a particular faith. These controls are not lessened by the fact that most of the lay teachers are of the Catholic faith. Inevitably some of a teacher's responsibilities hover on the border between secular and religious orientation.

The Court concluded that "[w]ith the best of intentions such a teacher would find it hard to make a total separation between secular teaching and religious doctrine."[30]

These conclusions by the Court in *Lemon* have come to be restated by the Court in case after case involving freedom of religious choice in education, culminating, perhaps, in the majority opinion of Justice Brennan in the 1985 case of *Aguilar v. Felton*.[31] There the Court invalidated use by New York City of federal funds to pay salaries of public employees who offered Title I, non-curricular services on Catholic school premises to meet the needs of educationally deprived children from low-income families. The program, in operation for nineteen years, was held to infringe "interests at the heart of the Establishment Clause", since state agents would have to ensure that the state teachers would not succumb to "the subtle or overt presence of religious matter in Title I classes".[32] A particular evil was found to lie in the administrative cooperation needed in order to provide the program:

> Administrative personnel of the public and parochial school systems must work together in resolving matters related to schedules, classroom assignments, problems that arise in the implementation of the program, requests for additional services, and the dissemination of information regarding the program.[33]

In a companion decision related to a similar issue handed down the same day, the Court, to the same effect, invented the "symbolic link" doctrine:

... the programs may provide a crucial symbolic link between government and religion, thereby enlisting—at least in the eyes of impressionable youngsters—the powers of government to the support of the religious denomination operating the school.[34]

The effect of all of this upon orthodox Catholics is to render them suspect persons. Suspicions will decrease to the extent that Catholics depart from orthodoxy and seek an image of total compatibility with secularism. But the faithful will continue to bear the legal stigmata of their Faith unless and until, at the highest level of judicial power, true constitutionalism takes hold.

3. *Right To Life Question.* The education decisions of the Supreme Court have been less significant in their effect upon Catholics in our society than have its decisions on abortion and (especially very recently) euthanasia (in its various degrees). At this hour all acknowledge that American society has moved into a great divide. The contest over the right to life is a contest for the soul of the nation and for its future.

Orthodox Catholics, in the 1950s, 1960s and 1970s were almost the sole opponents of abortion and of its legalization. They, more than any other body of citizens today, are chiefly identified in the public consciousness as defenders of the right to life. *Roe v. Wade*[35] and its successor decisions inevitably propelled orthodox Catholics not merely into resistance to the abortion movement but to all-out war against it. It is the *Catholic* presence in that war, more than any other presence, which has produced a wave of specifically anti-Catholic media expression such as may turn out to be unmatched in the history of the Church in this country. The more the terrifying implications of the anti-life movement (now tightly bound into radical feminism and the gay-lesbian movement) are felt, the more Catholics (I mean faithful Catholics) feel isolated from a culture which is coming, before their very eyes, to be utterly alien to them. We are truly beginning to experience life in an occupied country and are groping for the path ahead.

I need not elaborate on this particular effect of court decisions upon Catholics. I have but three conclusions to present in reaction to all of this.

First, we should take comfort in the fact that at least we are not alone. On the fronts of religious liberty, the parental right to religious education, and the right to life, we now have the welcome ally of "orthodox" Evangelicals. Whether we are welcome in their company or not (but often indeed we are), we should embrace them, that we may mutually lend strength to the efforts in the public forum which must be made if chaos is to be headed off and a good society had. Eighteen "orthodox" Catholics and Evangelicals have recently joined in a manifesto entitled *In Search of a National Morality*, co-published by the Evangelical Baker Book House and the Catholic Ignatius Press. Because of my respect for what these authors say, I commend it to your attention, albeit I am its editor.

My second conclusion pertains to the responsibilities of the Catholic bishops. The Church should be ultimately our hope for the creating of a virtuous (and thus just and peaceable) society for the future. But to that end, in the face of the now intense cultural (essentially religious) crisis, the leaders of the Church must insist on doctrinal fidelity, *must* by public action expose as un-Catholic those politicians who scandalize the faithful by public denials of their Church's teachings, and must decide whether they prefer the solidarity and unity of the Catholic people to the allowing of further destabilizing changes in the liturgy and religious practice. It is surely time for a moratorium on change, for a cessation of lingual perfectionism which, for many, lifts the anchors of the known and believed—and sets convictions afloat in a sea of uncertainty.

Finally: even this past week I have had rather numbing conversations with brothers and sisters of the Faith—and also with Evangelicals close to us—who say "Whatever is to become of us, the way things are heading?" They note that, of a sudden, or so it seems, great centers of power have been captured by militant secularists—the American Bar Association, the Democratic Party, NEA, all the major media. My ultimate response comes to my lips as I recall my days—eons ago—as an altar boy:

> Spera in Deo, quoniam adhuc confitebor illi:
> salutare vultus mei, et Deus meus.[36]

Postscript

I have studied with appreciation the papers presented by my colleagues on the general subject of "When Conscience and Politics Meet: A Catholic View". In different ways, each has pointed to the great underlying need which Catholics, on behalf of the whole society, face. All concur that, as we enter 1993, our society is mortally threatened, that it can be saved only by men and women of virtue, and that concentrating on promoting social programs will not only not produce a virtuous society but may bypass the achieving of such a society. Dr. Kirk, Dr. Hittinger, Dr. Hitchcock, Mrs. Bork, Father Canavan and Dr. Benestad have here all begged the Church to return to its essential work, the spiritual.

Why, then, would an attorney be given a role in these proceedings? Let me say at once that, these days, it is a great honor for any attorney to be invited to appear among decent people. That aside, I should speak of what I see as the function of Christian attorneys: to do what they can to bear into the world of the political the gifts created by the labor of our theologians, philosophers, historians, and other Christian scholars. We lawyers are not creators. We are the mechanics who try to translate the creators' work into features of the public order. And we have a second role to play—that is, to go to some places where the creators may not go, in combat for the good.

NOTES

[1] I have deliberately departed from the terms of the given title of this chapter by addressing, not the effect of judicial decisions on the *place* of Catholics in our society, since I see no such effect. Rather, I have thought it highly useful to comment simply on the effect of the decisions upon Catholics.

[2] The Roman emperor Decius, in the year 250, seeing threats of invasion from the north and violent revolution within, struggled, as Gibbon relates, "with the violence of the tempest, his mind, calm and amidst the tumult . . . , investigated the general causes that, since the age of the Antonines, had so impetuously urged the decline of Roman greatness". "He soon discovered", Gibbon continues, "that it was impossible to replace that greatness on a permanent basis without restoring public virtue, ancient principles and manners, and the oppressed majesty of the laws." He found, however, that "it was easier to vanquish both than to eradicate the public vices." E. Gibbon, I, *The Decline and Fall of the Roman Empire*, 216.

[3] Abraham Lincoln, First Inaugural Address, March 4, 1861, in 6 Richardson, *Messages and Papers of the Presidents*, 5, 9–10 (1897).

[4] See A. P. Stokes, II, *Church and State in the United States*, pp. 54–55.

[5] *Bradfield v. Roberts*, 175 U.S. 291 (1899); *Quick Bear v. Leapp*, 210 U.S. 50 (1908); *Cochran v. Board of Education*, 281 U.S. 370 (1930).

[6] 330 U.S. 1 (1947).

[7] See, e.g., R. L. Cord, *Separation of Church and State: Historical Fact and Current Fiction* (1982).

[8] 392 U.S. 236 (1968).

[9] 403 U.S. 602 (1971).

[10] 413 U.S. 756 (1973).

[11] 421 U.S. 349 (1975).

[12] 473 U.S. 373 (1985).

[13] 473 U.S. 402 (1985).

[14] 403 U.S. 672 (1971).

[15] Id. at 672, 687 (1971).

[16] 426 U.S. 736 (1976).

[17] Id. at 751.

[18] Id. at 755, 756.

[19] For examples of successful resistance to such impositions see *Wisconsin v. Yoder*, 406 U.S. 205 (1972); *State of Ohio v. Whisner*, 470 Ohio St. 2d 181 (1976); *Kentucky State Board of Education v. Rudasill*, 589 S.W. 2d 877 (Ky. 1979) *cert. denied*, 446 U.S. 938 (1980).

[20] See Pennsylvania Compulsory Attendance Law, 24 P.S. §13–1327.

[21] 330 U.S. 1, 21 (1947).

[22] Id. at 23–24.

[23] Id. at 24.

[24] 403 U.S. 602 (1971).

[25] P. Freund, Comment: Public Aid to Parochial Schools, 82 *Harv. L. Rev.* 1680 (1969).

[26] 403 U.S. at 622.

[27] Id. at 622, 623.

[28] Id. at 623.

[29] Ibid.

[30] Id. at 618, 619.

[31] 473 U.S. 402 (1985).

[32] Id. at 413.

[33] Ibid.

[34] *Grand Rapids School District v. Ball*, 473 U.S. 373, 390 (1985).

[35] 410 U.S. 113 (1973).

[36] From Psalm 41: "Hope in God, for I will still give praise to Him, the salvation of my countenance and my God."

JAMES HITCHCOCK

CATHOLICS IN THE PUBLIC SQUARE:
ISSUES FOR THE 1990S

The decade of the 1980s was one of the great moments of lost opportunity in the history of American Catholicism, an opportunity which may never come again.

The opportunity itself was ironic, in that it was provided by the triumph of the Republican Party, an institution traditionally thought of as non-Catholic at best and at times perhaps even anti-Catholic, while its great political rival had been one of the principal vehicles by which Catholics had been assimilated into American life and had achieved a high measure of political power.

Conventional wisdom holds that, as working-class people enter the ranks of the middle class and become prosperous, they tend to become Republican and conservative, and to some extent that has happened to Catholics. But the irony of the Catholic move to Republicanism around 1980 was that much of this was by working-class people who did not even feel comfortable with their new Republican allies and perhaps harbored serious reservations about Republican economic philosophy.

This occurred because what it meant to be a Democrat had also been changing since the mid-1960s. Among his other achievements, John F. Kennedy made the Democratic Party seem the party of fashion and no longer merely of "ordinary people." For over thirty years liberal ideology, and liberal political involvement, have seemed glamorous and stylish, their conservative opposites at best faintly stodgy. For this reason if no other, some newly prosperous Catholics have been pulled back into the Democratic Party at least as forcefully as they have been pulled toward Republicanism.

But the ideology of liberalism has itself been perceived as stylish—glamorous fund-raising balls chaired by entertainers expressing concern for the homeless, AIDS victims, and endangered species of animals, the enthusiasms of those who seem truly active as opposed to the mere repetition of homey orthodoxies on the other side.

The Reagan Era came as a great surprise to enlightened students of American culture, since it seemed to represent the triumph of forces judged to be already spent, at best rear-guard movements unable to cope with the modern world. Not only was the triumph of conservatism itself a surprise, its ideological accompaniments—in journalism, in the Washington "think tanks", and in numerous other places—itself showed an energy, an originality, and a youthfulness which had been regarded as almost a contradiction in terms.

Catholics were among those so taken by surprise by this that they were unable to accept it as anything other than a frustratingly mysterious revival of dead and discredited ideas to which no enlightened person could possibly subscribe. Catholic Democratic politicians can scarcely be blamed for not becoming Republicans. Their truly catastrophic failure was their acquiescence in the process by which the moral traditionalism of the Democratic Party was severed from its economic liberalism, to the point where many of its natural constituents felt that they had been driven out of the party. Not only did leading Catholic politicians, with rare exceptions, not oppose the dominance of the party by the fashionable left, in most instances they supported it enthusiastically.

The ostensible justification for this is if anything worse than the action itself, since it amounts to a disenfranchising not only of Catholics but of all seriously religious people—the contention that religion is a "personal" or "private" matter which should not "intrude" itself into the public arena. Numerous critics have exposed the incoherence of this contention, and its radical departure from even the recent past, the same people who not only welcomed but demanded the conspicuous participation of the churches in the Civil Rights movement now insisting that such political involvement is dangerous to the nation.

The specific issues over which Catholics have felt excluded from the Democratic Party need no enumeration, abortion being by far the most obvious and the most serious. What needs rather to be addressed is the liberal position which would effectively muzzle all those who claim any kind of religious warrant for their political beliefs, and who believe that a religiously based morality has a legitimate place in the dialogue.

The number of people who can be called secular humanists seems to be growing, and an overtly anti-religious philosophy is becoming increasingly acceptable. In the major liberal newspapers of the country scarcely a day elapses without either an essay or a letter from a reader insisting feverishly that "the religious right" is the chief danger to the country and that religious believers are evil people.

But such overt secularists are still a small minority of the population and would in themselves constitute no particular threat. But many at least nominal religious believers, especially liberal politicians, have themselves adopted the philosophy of secular humanism, and it is often purveyed to the public not by those who might arouse suspicion and alarm but by those who use their own religious credentials to allay such suspicions. It is far better, from a secular humanist standpoint, that this philosophy be presented to the public by Governor Mario Cuomo than by Norman Lear.

But the eager participation of so many Catholic politicians in the disenfranchisement of religious believers was not their work alone, and possibly could not have occurred without the active cooperation of people in official Church circles during the 1980s. Briefly put; sometime in the late 1960s the official Catholic bureaucracies at the national level essentially adopted almost the entire liberal Democratic program as their own, and have been faithful to that commitment ever since.

This too needs little rehearsal, for those who recall the bishops' official letters on war and peace and on the economy, to say nothing of the literally uncountable number of statements on every kind of public issue which national Catholic bodies have issued over a twenty-five year period.

The Church has of course remained firmly opposed to abortion, and has invested a great deal of moral capital and energy in the struggle against it. But the theory conventionally called the "seamless garment", most comprehensively defined by Cardinal Joseph Bernardin of Chicago, has effectively undercut that commitment at numerous points. As a practical matter, it has left Catholics with no meaningful guidance in determining their votes, since usually they face a choice between candidates both of whom seem to address some of the "life issues", as the Church bureaucracy defines them, but not others.

More importantly, the "seamless garment" formula, and the entire thrust of Catholic social teaching as defined at the national level, makes the abortion issue seem anomalous. If true humanitarianism, and indeed even true understanding of the Gospel, points to public figures like Governor Cuomo, Senator Edward Kennedy, and Father Robert Drinan for leadership, how is it possible to think that they have gone badly wrong on a single issue? In countless ways American Catholics have been encouraged by their national leaders to view the world essentially through the glasses of the left wing of the Democratic Party, a view in which abortion inevitably seems an oddity at best, and ultimately a terrible misjudgment.

If the legacy of the Kennedy years has made liberal ideology seem irresistibly glamorous to many assimilated Catholics, the stance of the national Church leadership has made that ideology seem also like the genuine expression of Catholic thought, to the point where those who are too exercised about abortion can even be viewed as flawed in their Catholicism, unwilling to follow the "opening to the world" supposedly decreed by the Second Vatican Council.

Superficially the activities of the national Catholic bureaucracy seem to disprove strongly the claim that religion has no legitimate place in public life, to the point where it often seems that the staff of the United States Catholic Conference have made religion if anything too intrusive in the political process. But this is misleading because, deliberately or otherwise, that leadership commits itself to issues which already have the approval of a broad liberal consensus, including most of those people who insist that religion does not belong in public life.

The political role of the Church is thus reduced to that of a cheering section for movements virtually all of which have originated elsewhere, from secular roots, which depend mainly on secular movements for their strength and energy, and which feel no need for theological justification. All but the most fanatical secularists are willing to accept a Church which plays this role, even as they issue dire warnings, and even threats, when the Church dares to proclaim a moral position for which there is little secular support.

Although liberal Catholics claim to be motivated by the highest considerations of religious principle, this is seldom evident at points where faith might make a measurable difference, precisely issues like abortion. This being the case, the expressed "faith commitments" of Catholics like Governor Cuomo cannot help but seem like religious embellishments added to positions already formulated in accord with secular principles.

For many American Catholics "coming of age" in the 1960s was partially validated by their adoption of a left-liberal view of the world. If even liberal Catholics before 1960 were characterized by, among other things, anti-Communism and conservatism on what are now called "the social issues", many self-consciously "Vatican II Catholics" have felt almost a compulsion to embrace the anti-war movement, including its anti-American manifestations, as well as the pro-abortion movement and numerous other forces of moral iconoclasm. Today many assimilated Catholics would feel highly uncomfortable being labelled "conservative" on any issue whatsoever.

But even as this kind of assimilation was occurring, there

was an almost unnoticed "coming of age" of other American Catholics, in other ways. The movement of Catholics toward the Republican Party ought at least to be seen as evidence of a political independence previously absent. More important, Catholics had the political will and ability to force a party previously hostile or indifferent to their needs to embody a good part of a distinctively Catholic program in its own platform.

Public figures like William Bennett and Justice Antonin Scalia can in many ways be seen as representing the flowering of an authentically Catholic view of the world, not only on specific matters like abortion but in terms of a developed, confident sense of the need for political society to rest on an ordered moral foundation with traditional roots, the mirror opposite of the moral agnosticism which now drives political liberalism.

But the tragedy of this is the fact that, at precisely the moment in American history when such a vision of society could for the first time be effectively expressed by prominent Catholics, the national Church leadership contrived to make it seem the product of a retarded faith.

The first great missed opportunity of the 1980s was the failure of Catholics within the Democratic Party to fight the battle for moral conservatism. According to the usual laws of politics, one of the major internal tensions within the party over the past quarter century should have been between traditionally Democratic Catholics, led by men like Governor Cuomo, and the phenomenon sometimes dubbed "radical chic", a tension which, had there been sufficient will to endure it, would probably have resulted in a victory for the moral traditionalists. Instead Catholic Democratic politicians, with rare and honorable exceptions like Governor Robert Casey of Pennsylvania, eagerly acquiesced in the disenfranchisement of their own people, an act which may be without precedent in American history.

The second missed opportunity has already been indicated —the refusal of the national Church leadership to make even a loose alliance with the emerging Republican majority, with the Reagan-Bush administration. During the Reagan years, one of the open secrets of Washington life was the prevalence of articulate, committed Catholics in the White House, the various government agencies, and the "think tanks". But without exception all of those people felt rebuffed by the national Church leadership, their very existence a kind of embarrassment to the image of the Church this leadership wished to project.

Catholic political witness can never be simply an alliance with a particular party, and the shift of Catholics toward the Republicans was primarily forced on them by the actions of the Democrats rather than by any deliberate decision on their part. Inevitably, the Republican Party itself has failed in significant ways. Thus the presence of committed Catholics within the government seems to have diminished measurably during the Bush administration, and the president has often managed to emit mixed signals about the basic moral issues, seeming not so much to reject conservative positions as not to understand them fully, or not to understand why they are important.

But beyond the particular issues, even the weakened Republican Party of the 1990s still grants a home to those who think religious principles should guide political action. Besides that, the conservatism of the Republican Party in the sense of its ideological inertia, makes it far less dangerous to principled Catholics than is the Democratic Party, in that Republicans, because of their opposition to "big government", are far less likely to begin new programs, heavily funded and with large bureaucracies, which use the power of government to determine the country's moral direction (for example, through the mandatory distribution of condoms in schools and mandatory classes which seek to legitimize immoral sexual behavior, which are now often done by liberal governments on the local level).

The almost certain defeat of the Republicans in 1992 will unleash a civil war for the soul of the party. One explanation already being offered for the party's failure is its connections with the "religious right", which allegedly constitutes only a small and eccentric, but still dangerous, element abhorrent to the mainstream of the citizenry. There are no doubt Republican leaders who find, or profess to find, that a persuasive explanation. Should the forces of an older Republicanism, the kind which for decades merely echoed Democratic ideas somewhat more faintly, regain ascendancy in the party, Catholics would find themselves without any political home at all.

The 1990s are likely to be a grim decade for American Catholics under any circumstances, much of that because, if ideological liberals are once more in the ascendancy, there will be powerful, even fanatical, efforts to implement an agenda which many liberals feel has been illegitimately blocked since 1969. The legacy of the New Left and the Counter-Culture are strong indeed in the Democratic Party, and that suppressed legacy includes comprehensive plans for eradicating the last remains of moral traditionalism, as illustrated by Hillary Clinton's notion of "children's rights", for example. The dominant groups within liberalism are zealously committed to various kinds of social engineering, based on the assumption that certified experts and their bureaucratic allies understand best what is good for the American people.

Thus, the "issue" of the 1990s goes far beyond any particular issues like abortion, while including those issues, for the Democratic Party has simply made itself the party of modernity in all its fullness, committed irretrievably to the political unfolding of the modernist agenda of deep scepticism toward all received wisdom, indifference, or outright hostility to traditional institutions like the family, eagerness to use government power to promote every kind of iconoclastic effort. (Thus the activities of the National Endowment for the Arts, while only a tiny part of the Federal government's total budget, are a telling index of the moral orientation of the government at any particular moment.)

Contemporary liberalism does far more than simply ask citizens to tolerate abortion, homosexuality, anti-religious art, and many other things which offend their beliefs, it further requires that these same citizens surrender the right to make any moral judgment at all. Toleration is urged not on the basis of accommodating things of which one might disapprove but of having no basis on which even to make such a judgment. The battle for laws and public policy becomes, therefore, a continuing referendum on the very possibility of moral truth.

The liberalism of the 1990s, including some Republicans, will continue moving toward what can be called benign totalitarianism—the steady expansion of law and government to claim jurisdiction over more and more aspects of people's lives, including things hitherto thought to be private and personal, such as the raising of children.

In this benign totalitarianism there is a role for religion as an ideological support for an enlightened government. But in principle, according to liberal ideology, religion cannot and will not be allowed to make claims of its own.

The Church is always a teaching institution and only indirectly a political one and, especially given its likely exclusion from effective politics during the 1990s, it might seem the better part of wisdom to concentrate on that teaching duty to the exclusion of politics. But in modern America effective teaching on moral issues is not possible without some kind of public program which can inspire action. Sermons about abortion will have little effect if their hearers have no tangible ways to apply those teachings.

So long as the new liberal ascendancy lasts, Catholics will find little opportunity for aggressive political action in the 1990s. Instead they will probably have to concentrate on defensive actions in support of whatever gains they achieved in the previous decade, and in resistance to what will probably be a massive attack on traditional beliefs in the public sphere—the expansion of abortion to a universal and totally unrestricted right, systematic extension of homosexual rights supported by the full power of the government, steady pressure on the independence of the churches through government regulations and threats against tax exemption.

As already suggested, the vulnerability of the Church in American life is as much the result of its internal problems as of the forces of secularism itself. In this respect nothing is more dangerous than the willingness of certain liberal politicians, notably Governor Cuomo, to offer themselves as spiritual leaders, in effect suggesting to assimilated Catholics that they place their trust in their politicians rather than in their anointed spiritual leaders. (Thus Governor Cuomo expounds publicly on the theological revolution allegedly wrought by Pierre Teilhard de Chardin.)

At the level of the episcopacy the Church in the United States has been slowly moving toward stronger and more vigorous leadership since about the mid-1980s, and it is crucial that this movement accelerate. Nothing could be more damaging than a reversion to an episcopal leadership prepared to acquiesce quietly in the disenfranchisement of the Catholic people. (Such disenfranchisement could be concealed by a practice of endorsing enthusiastically most of the programs of the newly restored liberalism, thus creating the illusion that the Church is an important force in public life.)

One of the elements making possible the "Reagan Revolution" was the unexpected rise of a politically militant conservative Protestantism, as encapsulated in the Moral Majority. But Jerry Falwell's organization, which once struck terror in so many liberal hearts, is now defunct, and it appears that the evangelical-fundamentalist political presence is diminishing overall.

To a degree unrecognized by most Catholics, this conservative Protestant upsurge provided a kind of protective covering for Catholics, making it impossible to dismiss abortion, for example, as merely a "Catholic issue". Indeed, in time most secularists seemed to come to regard organized conservative Protestantism as a greater danger than organized Catholicism, a protective covering some national Catholic leaders were perhaps grateful to be able to use.

To the degree that morally conservative positions such as

opposition to abortion became respectable in the 1980s, much of that respectability was due to their official espousal at the highest levels of national life—it was difficult to dismiss, as merely crazy or eccentric positions which the president of the United States, and many highly articulate officials, publicly espoused. During much of the 1990s that situation is likely to be reversed, and there will be determined efforts to exclude moral traditionalists even from the public debate, on the grounds that they represent a retrograde and even dangerous minority position.

Catholics will play a crucial role here whether or not conservative Protestantism is in decline, because Catholics are better equipped than Protestants to carry on the discussion in "neutral" terms rather than merely by direct appeals to religious authority which will be rejected out of hand. Properly understood, in fact, Catholics do not appeal to religious authority at all for their public positions but to a sense of the common good open to examination by reason and empirical evidence. Thus during the 1990s a major Catholic task will be to keep alive an awareness of the measurable ill effects of morally misguided public policy, and the cures offered by morally sound policy.

The return of the liberals to national power during the 1990s itself illustrates a dimension of the political situation which even most traditional Catholics have not addressed systematically—the tendency since at least 1933 to view government, and especially the presidency, as the ultimate guarantor of national prosperity.

Superficially, traditional Catholic social thought often seemed to support that view, in that it has generally supported some version of the welfare state, by which government provides for those whose needs cannot otherwise be met. But this principle has gradually shaded into the unexamined conviction, accepted publicly by President Bush as well as by Governor William Clinton, that the success or failure of a government can and ought to be assessed primarily on the basis of the country's economic health.

There are growing doubts as to how much government can in fact accomplish, whether the forces which shape the economy are not ultimately beyond effective political control. But besides those doubts, the predominantly economic approach to politics is literally materialistic, an approach which demands that people suppress their fears concerning the moral health of the country in exchange for a promise of greater prosperity.

Classical social theory predicated that a democratically pluralistic society would inevitably produce a radically democratized morality, in which everyone's opinion is necessarily as good as everyone else's and in which no moral absolute of any kind can be validly asserted. Until now the United States has been a living historical refutation of that warning. The ultimate political battle of the 1990s centers on precisely that prediction —is it still possible to think that a truly democratic, and truly pluralistic, society can base itself on firm moral principles, even when not all its citizens agree on those principles?

Ultimately, of course, government can guarantee the country's moral health even less than it can guarantee economic prosperity. But, as conservative Protestants pointed out when they began to get politically active for the first time, it is impossible to remain quiescent when the full power of government is being used to effect moral revolution. American Catholics are now entering, at least temporarily, a political wilderness. Their safe emergence a few years hence is crucial to the well being of both the Church and the nation.

MARY ELLEN BORK

THE CATHOLIC PUBLIC
SERVANT UNDER PRESSURE:
MEN AND WOMEN OF PRINCIPLE

William Butler Yeats' poem "The Second Coming", written in 1919, uses the image of a center that cannot hold, an image often quoted to describe the state of our culture today. His poetic image captures the idea of dissolution and loss of recognizable shape of Western culture as the influence of the Judeo-Christian tradition weakens. He writes:

> "Turning and turning in the widening gyre
> The falcon cannot hear the falconer;
> Things fall apart; 'the centre cannot hold'
> Mere anarchy is loosed upon the world,
> The blood-dimmed tide is loosed, and everywhere
> The ceremony of innocence is drowned;
> The best lack all conviction, while the worst
> Are full of passionate intensity."[1]

It ends with "And what rough beast, its hour come round at last, Slouches towards Bethlehem to be born." The image of a center not holding suggests a spinning away from the core, a source of meaning. Many would agree the image aptly fits the direction of some cultural trends, the disintegration of age-old institutions like the family, and in its place the claim by other groupings of equal legitimacy; the increase in drug use, violence, inner-city poverty, divorce, homosexuality, pedophilia, and, closer to home, the increase in Catholic school closings. Looking at all this, my husband has decided to write a book about the culture with a working title of "Slouching Towards Gomorrah".

In Oregon people will vote in November on whether or not homosexuality should be approved and tolerated or disapproved and discouraged. Children are taking their parents to court in search of better care and the Supreme Court ruled this term in favor of a teenager who was offended by a prayer said by a rabbi at her graduation. Prayer at public school graduations is now banned by the highest court in the land for fear that it promotes the establishment of religion.

More than anarchy in a political sense is suggested by Yeats' image. In a society where "the best lack all conviction while the worst are full of passionate intensity" a sense of truth and commitment to that truth are lacking as well as a sense of direction, of purpose, "the vision thing". If we have no conviction about what is true, no acceptance of objective moral standards, a moral anarchy reigns. Democracy as we know it is gradually altered, human life is held cheap, the individual self reigns without moral constraints and the religion is looked upon as irrelevant.

Enter the Catholic public servant. Formed by a tradition that sees service in public life as a form of charity, a way of promoting the common good and seeking justice for all, the Catholic public servant is challenged at every turn today because the culture war is out in the open. The Catholic understanding of the dignity of each person, the value of human life, and the common good of society is rooted in belief in God. This "traditional value" is no longer shared by the whole people. Pope John Paul II, so acutely aware of this situation, urges on us "the pressing responsibility" to "bear witness to those human and gospel values that are intimately connected with political activity itself, such as liberty and justice, solidarity, faithful and unselfish dedication for the good of all, a simple life-style and a preferential love for the poor and the least."[2] To communicate this attitude in a political scene that is ever more cynical and hostile to things spiritual, requires true virtue and a well-formed conscience, and an ability to articulate that stand, and integrity. The political pressure is great to conform, to be less "prejudiced" and more "tolerant".

In this paper I would like to look at the kind of pressure Catholic leaders have to deal with today, examine a sampling of responses by leading Catholics, and see the lessons we can learn from the sixteenth century layman St. Thomas More about deciding who we are, following our conscience and doing what is right no matter what the cost.

In the last twenty years we have witnessed the phenomenon of Catholic politicians caving in to the pressure of the secular cultural elites on a grand scale. Starting with the election of the first Catholic president, Kennedy, who assured us that his faith would not interfere with his public life, we have seen many politicians go along with the prevailing view that religion is a private matter and has little place in the public square. At a time when Catholic public servants are positioned to stand for traditional and religious values, people like Mario Cuomo, Daniel Patrick Moynihan, and Teddy Kennedy have chosen to promote the idea that a Catholic can have private beliefs that do not influence their public moral stands. They have succumbed to social and political pressure and caved in on the most important moral question of the day and yet cling to their identity as Catholics. They see nuance where there can be none. A few have not succumbed to this pressure (may their tribe increase) and stand in the tradition of Thomas More, the Catholic public servant who weighed the choices put before him in terms of earthly good and eternal good without confusing the two.

That public servants face pressure is nothing new. Anyone who runs for office and accepts political responsibility will face the challenge of making good policy and be tempted to do what is politically expedient, but not morally right. In our day the stakes are higher than ever because the culture war pits two views against each other about fundamental questions of religious values, the individual, the community, freedom, and democratic society. One view sees a naked public square with a privatized view of religion; the other sees a public square informed and supported by traditional religious and moral values. Those Catholics who have adopted the progressive view often dismiss the moral teaching of the Church in favor of being politically correct. Under pressure they quiet their conscience by obfuscating moral issues and sounding tolerant.

The general attitude used to be that "most Americans don't mix politics and religion much, as long as their candidates reflect a kind of 'generic Christianity' that mirrors their own views and isn't too startling."[3] Now all manner of values are competing in the public forum for attention and approval from distribution of condoms in schools to homosexual marriages. The Supreme Court has sided with the liberal side of the culture war. As the Christian consensus disappears, the time is ripe for Catholic politicians to defend the values they cherish.

A Catholic public servant who is faithful to the Church and to traditional moral values experiences two kinds of pressure, cultural and moral on the one hand and spiritual on the other. The cultural pressure comes from the political community in which he works as well as from sections of the Catholic community who have accepted the positions of the dominant culture. Interestingly this war is not being waged between institutions any more but across institutional lines so that some members of the Catholic and evangelical churches find they have more in common with each other in their acceptance of traditional values than with members of their own church. This realignment among institutions in the culture makes for new and different allies in defending traditional values than was the case thirty years ago.

This makes Democrat Governor Casey criticize his party for their unreasonable intolerance of any position but pro-abortion. He was silenced at the Democratic convention which proclaims a "politics of inclusion" and recently in New York where he was to speak on "Can a liberal be pro-life?" For thirty-five minutes abortion advocates and street crazies screamed and chanted "Racist, sexist, anti-gay, Governor Casey go away."[4] He never got to speak. Ever since my husband's nomination the nastiness and brutality of the liberal opposition has reached new lows. They will stop at nothing to achieve their goal, even character assassination, complete distortion of one's record, and hostility to free speech for pro-lifers, especially if they are Catholic.

The second kind of pressure a Catholic politician deals with is of a spiritual nature, affecting the soul. It takes many forms from the temptation to busyness that distracts a good person from seeking spiritual maturity, to the timidity and hesitation which inhibits one from witnessing to gospel values in the market place. When faith is weak, the consideration of eternal verities is weak. The crisis of faith today shows itself in many ways, among them giving in to the idea that religion is private, that it is a compartment which we open on Sunday and close on Monday. In order to witness to the gospel the life of virtue has to be vibrant, allowing ourselves to be transformed by gospel values, discerning God's action in our lives, withstanding temptation and fear in order to follow our well-informed conscience. For the politician to stand for human and gospel values, that have been clarified and tested by the Church, and are at the heart of the democratic society envisioned by our founding fathers, requires real virtue.

St. Thomas More, often called the man of singular virtue, has much to teach us in this matter. He experienced cultural and spiritual pressures of pre-Reformation England which culminated with his refusal to sign an oath that would negate his understanding and allegiance to his Catholic Faith. He was the only layman not to sign as John Fisher was the only bishop. He was a friend of the King since childhood and knew well all the leaders of his day who pressured him to do what seemed to them such a small thing to maintain his place of honor. Thomas More withstood this pressure because he saw clearly what was at stake. The oath would mean denying his Catholic Faith and he saw the eternal dimension of this choice. He was bound by his conscience to follow what he saw as truth. His strength under pressure came from his spiritual life which informed his life of political responsibility as a lawyer, judge, and Chancellor of England under King Henry VIII. Prayer was a vital part of his daily life and that of his family. When his time of testing came amid the rumblings of the Reformation he deepened his life with God, prayed, and wrestled with his fear. When he finally went to the scaffold his wit never left him. He asked for help going up the wooden platform commenting that he needed assistance going up but would not need any coming down. The executioner was weeping and he comforted him telling him that they would be merry in heaven and saying, "I die the King's good servant but God's first."

The problem today is that many Catholic politicians have lost their grasp of the truth and settle for a modern relativist position espoused by the modern liberals. One hears echoes of Pilate's perplexed question to Jesus, "What is truth?" as we listen to the careful distinctions offered by some in present-ing their "nuanced" position on religion and politics. Cuomo admitted in his 1984 Notre Dame talk that he did not like "tal-ismanic criteria" and "simplistic answers".[5] For him the matter of how much religion influences a politician's decisions is an area of prudential judgment. He is convinced that he cannot impose his moral conviction that abortion is wrong on others. This is the path of political realism and tolerance. He thinks laws against abortion do not work because people will con-tinue to want abortions. So he continues to support Medicaid funding for abortion even though the Federal government does not allow it. He takes refuge in the fact that many Catholics are pro-abortion. He thinks those who are pro-life and those who are pro-choice can work together for "government pro-grams that present an impoverished mother with the full range of support she needs to bear and raise her children".[6]

Both Cuomo and Kennedy seem more impressed by the fact that they live in a pluralistic culture and need to be tolerant than by the importance of discerning the truth and defending it. The greatest sin for them is intolerance. Kennedy's ill-conceived fear is that if Catholic leaders take a strong moral stand government may become an agent of religion. By not defending traditional moral values our government has become an agent for religion, that of secular humanism over and against the Judeo-Christian religions.

A few Catholic voices are raised that see the problem clearly. For Henry Hyde, congressman from Illinois, and Chris Smith, congressman from New Jersey, both up for re-election, the departure from the original understanding of separation of church and state in the last few decades has led to a virtual ruling out of religious values from the public arena. The dominant culture eschews positions influenced by faith and religious values. The abortion debate as carried on in the media and on television never speaks of a moral question but only a matter of freedom and choice for the individual woman. To ignore the moral dimension of this defining moral question for America cannot be done without impunity. The presence of Catholic and evangelical resistance to the impending spiritual vacuum is to be encouraged so that our country can find its way into the next century intact.

If we look again at St. Thomas More in April 1534, he was not with a crowd of Catholics refusing to sign. He was alone in refusing to take the oath required of all adults to support the new Act of Succession which said that the marriage of Henry VIII and Catherine of Aragon was utterly void notwithstanding the Papal dispensation in reliance on which it had been entered upon twenty-five years before. Henry was determined to marry Ann Boleyn. Those who did not sign the Act were guilty of treason. Thomas had read all the documents and had informed the King earlier that he could find nothing to support the King's position. In a letter to Thomas Cromwell from the Tower explaining the history of his involvement in this issue, More was at pains to point out that he was not being obstinate and had no desire to displease the King. He asked Cromwell to tell the King about his "true faithful mind", his fault "that I cannot in everything think the same way that some other men of more wisdom and deeper learning do. . . ."[7]

In November of 1534 a second Act was passed which included the words "abjure any foreign potentate" which meant renouncing the authority of the pope. He again refused to take the oath because by doing so he would "imperil my soul to perpetual damnation".[8] Why did he think differently than other men?

More was clear that truth was on one side and that truth is binding. He based his refusal on two judgments: that the marriage to Catherine was valid and in conformity with divine law and it would be wrong for Henry to disregard this, and that "to declare on oath that something is *not* the case when one actually judges that it *is* the case is to lie, which is always against divine law".[9] So More went to the Tower "because of a perfectly ordinary and universal (though specific) moral norm which excludes lying, most clearly under oath".[10]

He did not denounce those who came to a different conclusion having carefully considered the question of Henry's first marriage, but he recognized that they were following consciences that were influenced by political convenience and pride, and many were in bad faith. When the question of Henry's marriage was linked to renouncing the authority of the pope, the question of the oath took on much greater dimensions.

More was deeply concerned about the structure of the historic Christian Faith and would not stand with those who would tamper with it for the sake of private feelings. Over the years he spent many hours answering in writing those who proposed various heresies about Christianity because he knew the truth of the Catholic Faith would be tarnished thereby. His stand against Henry VIII was rooted in his love and deep understanding of the Church.

During his imprisonment in a stone cell carved out of rock about the size of a small hotel room in the Tower, More had to deal with fear that his physical nature might not be able to hold out until the end. He recognized this as temptation and dealt with it by writing several literary and spiritual works including *The Dialogue of Comfort against Tribulation.* The "comfort" meant here is not physical comfort but rather the spiritual comfort of the virtue of hope when faced with grave difficulties. More insists that our hope is rooted in "God's willingness to give us the strength to resist temptation so that we may at last attain the final object of our hope."[11]

His meditation on Psalm 90 reveals his approach to the fears that assailed him. They are the fears that assail any virtuous public servant under pressure. He shows how God's shield of truth protects us from four dangers mentioned in verses 5 and 6, "You shall not fear the terror of the night nor the arrow that flies by day; not the pestilence that roams in darkness nor the devastating plague at noon".

The terror of the night is the temptation to impatience, to being overwhelmed by fear itself, causing good men to lose the virtues of faith and hope. The arrow flying by day is the opposite temptation as day is opposite night; it is pride. More sees the arrow of pride striking in times of prosperity and when men have position and authority. The remedy is always hope in God which helps him to use his prosperity well because of trust in God's grace.

The third temptation, the pestilence that roams in the darkness, is covetousness for worldly things. Even good people are tempted to put their hearts in worldly possessions. When they have material goods, they can be preoccupied by this and the devil convinces them that they are not pleasing to God. They fret and are fearful. The fear itself draws our minds away from God and "from the spiritual consolation of good hope that he should have in God's help". Covetousness is not in the having but in "the will and desire and affection to have and the longing for"[12] riches. If we are surrounded by the truth of God we can avoid this temptation.

The fourth temptation, the devastating plague at noon, is the most deadly temptation, the fear of direct persecution and a painful death. More writes:

"Thus may we see that in such persecutions, it is the midday devil himself that maketh such incursion upon us, by the men that are his ministers to make us fall for fear. For till we fall, he can never hurt us. And therefore sayth St. Peter, *Resistite Diabolo et fugiet a vobis*, Stand against the devil and he shall fly from you, for he never runneth upon a man to seize on him with his claws, till he see him down on the ground willingly fallen himself, for his fashion is to set his surrogates against us, and by them to make us for fear or for impatience fall" "And himself in the meanwhile compasseth us, running and roaring like a rampant lion about us, looking who will fall, that he may devour him."[13]

The fear is twofold: a fear of pain and torture on the one hand and the enticement and promise of rest and quiet on the other. The defense for the faithful Christian is to reason clearly which leads to charity and hope in God's assistance. More's approach to temptation is primarily through his reason, which applies the theological richness of his Faith to his concrete situation.

Public servants would do well to learn from More the thoroughly Christian mind he brought into the public square and the importance of allowing oneself to be bound by the truth in all matters. Even in the face of vehement opposition More points the way to the source of true consolation and support for the Christian in faith, hope, and charity.

His choice brought him suffering which he understood as his participation in the suffering and death of Christ. Earlier in *A Dialogue Concerning Heresies*, he wrote explaining Christ's easy yoke:

"What ease also call you this, yet we be bounded to abide all sorrow and shameful death and all martyrdom upon pain of perpetual damnation for the profession of our faith. Think you that these easy words of his easy yoke and light burden were not as well spoken to his apostles as to you, and yet what ease called he them to. Called he not them to watching, fasting, praying, preaching, walking, hunger, thirst, cold, and heat, beating, scourging, prisonment, painful and shameful death. The ease of his yoke standeth not in bodily ease, nor the lightness of his burden standeth not in the slackness of any bodily pain (except we be so wanton, that where himself had not heaven without pain, we look to come thither with play) but it standeth in the sweetness of hope, whereby we feel in our pain a pleasant taste of heaven."[14]

Such strength of spirit and clear-mindedness seems to be in short supply today. We need to recover this side of the Catholic tradition, the spiritual depth and Christian thinking that formed the soul of this great man in order to be effective in the public square.

The experience of having one's integrity tested is the sifting process in which we recognize true leadership and sometimes saints. To be under pressure is a revealing moment for the leader and for those who look for leadership as it was for Thomas More, George Washington, or Abraham Lincoln. What is revealed is the presence of virtue, of prudence, discernment, fortitude, equanimity, balance or the lack of it.

I remember in my husband's nomination experience sitting in the Senate caucus room before the Judiciary Committee with bright lights, camera, and action. The greatest trial for both of us was the extent of the lying about Bob's record to his face by elected politicians like Kennedy and Metzenbaum before a national television audience. The relentless attack continued in the newspapers by radical interest groups working with Senator Kennedy. The charges against him were repeated for months. Bob thought that as a judge he should not be political so he did not personally answer many of the statements against him. The Republicans and the White House were painfully slow getting organized and when they did it was too late.

But grace abounded during that time. Bob's calm demeanor helped the family to focus on his responsibilities. He was fully aware of the political nature of the battle and never lost sight of his role as a judge during the entire process.

The Catholic public servant has a dual role: to fulfill his

responsibilities of leadership to the political community and to serve God in his heart. The interplay of spiritual strength and practical expertise are part of his service. Today's cultural climate does not support the person who stands for traditional and religious values as it did in the past. In order not to lose our grip on the purpose of it all, our spiritual sense of living in a world that is under divine guidance, we have to be spiritually strong.

What is it that inhibits a person from standing tall and doing what is right? It is the old story. St. Paul and St. Thomas More tell us the flesh wars against the spirit. The flesh is weak, hindering the spirit from pursuing the right. But we have a choice to make.

The challenge is to be persons of faith guided by the Holy Spirit at the heart of the world. St. Paul says in 1 Corinthians 2, 12–16, "The Spirit we have received is not the world's spirit, but God's Spirit helping us to recognize the gifts he has given us . . . interpreting spiritual things in spiritual terms. The natural man does not accept what is taught by the Spirit of God. For him, that is absurdity. He cannot come to know such teaching because it must be appraised in a spiritual way. The spiritual man, on the other hand, can appraise everything. . . . We have the mind of Christ."

I am haunted by the fact that Thomas More was alone in his decision not to sign the oath. Henry VIII was on the side of the culture war that affirmed his own individual will and gratification enforced by the political power of the Throne. More stood with the historic Catholic community defending its existence and its God-given mission. If more Catholics had stood with More, perhaps the cost to the Church would not have been so great. Many went over to Protestantism who would have stayed in the Church. The Catholic Church in England was decimated in its members, its monasteries, and its churches.

More was able to stand against the King because of his strength of character, his deep faith, his clear intellectual perception of the moral and religious issues involved, and his deep love of the Church. For this he experienced disapproval, ostracism, imprisonment, suffering, and death. And still he speaks to us 450 years later. Perhaps we should not be surprised that there are few good men and women of this singular character today. But I would rather not leave it there. We must hope that there are those with strong faith who will take the risk and enter the arena of politics on the side of traditional and religious values. Those persons will need the support of the rest of us and they will have it.

NOTES

[1] A. Norman Jeffares, *W. B. Yeats: A New Biography* (New York, 1988), p. 226.

[2] Pope John Paul II, *Christifideles laici* (Rome, 1988), 124.

[3] Stephen Goode, "The Spirit Can Still Move the Electorate", *Washington Times Magazine Insight* (August 30, 1992), p. 13.

[4] John Leo, "Shouted down . . . for life?," *The Washington Times* (October 14, 1992), G1.

[5] Mario Cuomo, "Religious Belief and Public Morality: A Catholic Governor's Perspective," *The New York Times* (September 16, 1984).

[6] Ibid.

[7] Elizabeth Frances Rogers, ed., *St. Thomas More: Selected Letters*, (New Haven, 1961), p. 215.

[8] Ibid., p. 227.

[9] John Finnis, "Thomas More and the Crisis in Faith and Morals," an address for the Thomas More Society, Melbourne (August 23, 1989), 12.

[10] Ibid., 3.

[11] St. Thomas More, *A Dialogue of Comfort Against Tribulation*, ed. by Louis L. Martz and Frank Manley (New Haven, 1976), xcvi.

[12] Ibid., civ.

[13] Ibid., cx.

[14] Ibid., clxiii.